se

stress,

**MAXIMISE
SUCCESS**

POSITIVE BUSINESS

minimise
stress,
MAXIMISE
SUCCESS

CLARE HARRIS

DUNCAN BAIRD PUBLISHERS

LONDON

Minimise Stress, Maximise Success
Clare Harris

First published in the United Kingdom and Ireland in 2003 by
Duncan Baird Publishers Ltd
Sixth Floor
Castle House
75–76 Wells Street
London W1T 3QH

Conceived, created and designed by Duncan Baird Publishers

Managing Editor: Judy Barratt
Editors: Ingrid Court-Jones with Hanne Bewernick
Managing Designer: Dan Sturges
Designer: 27.12 Design Ltd
Commissioned artwork: Ben Goss and Melvyn Evans

British Library Cataloguing-in-Publication Data:
A CIP record for this book is available from the British Library.

ISBN: 1-904292-16-X

1 3 5 7 9 10 8 6 4 2

Typeset in Bembo
Colour reproduction by Colourscan, Singapore
Printed in Singapore by Imago

For Digger, Tamsin and Anna, with love

CONTENTS

AUTHOR'S FOREWORD

This is a hugely exciting time for everyone who is interested in the extraordinary links that exist between the body and the mind, and what this means for us. An understanding of the "body-mind", which has existed for centuries in Eastern thinking, is now being proven scientifically in the West on a chemical, cellular level.

All my adult life, I've been interested in learning about tension – what makes people tense, what tension does to a person's feelings and performance and so on. This inevitably led me to investigate its opposite – relaxation. As a young teacher in school, I saw how anxiety in children could create a kind of mental paralysis which inhibited them from learning. I discovered that the key to transforming their progress lay in finding ways to relax the children and make them feel hopeful and confident.

Later, when I qualified in massage, and taught it for many years, I had the privilege of learning how diverse people's bodies are – each is unique. The more people I massaged, the more I realized that everyone has their own patterns of physical tension. I also studied bioenergetic therapy, which taught me that each of us has our own patterns of emotional tension, too, and that anxiety, fear or anger is mapped on to the body in a way that is readable by the bioenergetic therapist.

Later still, I qualified as an integrative counsellor. My training was good, but concentrated mostly on the mind and contained relatively little about the body. I found myself believing more and more that if working therapeutically with people was the right job for me, then the therapeutic journey should be a holistic one that included the whole person − not just the body in which they live, but also the mind, the heart and the soul. I felt (and still feel) blessed to work with people in this way.

Lecturing at Cranfield School of Management's Praxis Centre for Developing Personal Effectiveness, I became much more aware of the extra-ordinary pressure that is part of daily corporate life. With support and interest from wonderful colleagues at Praxis, I began developing programs that taught our delegates about the body-mind connection, and helped them understand and manage stress in a genuinely holistic way. My aim was to give them the tools to create their own realistic, workable interventions for both body and mind that would release chronic tension and help them build exceptional well-being. The response from delegates was incredibly positive.

I have come to have a deep respect and admiration for those of you (members of my own family included) who work in large business organizations. It takes energy, resilience, staying power and, often, courage. Everything in this book has been tried-and-tested with the business community − my heartfelt hope is that it will help you become stress-free, relaxed and self-aware so that you can realize your potential and maximize success.

HOW TO USE THIS BOOK

This book has five chapters, which together form a personal development guide that teaches practical, effective strategies for dealing successfully with the pressures of business life.

Chapter 1 explores how stress impacts on us at work, examining how it affects both our body and our mind. It takes a look at common causes of stress in the workplace and teaches us how to evaluate our major stressors.

Chapter 2 focuses on how stress can influence our thinking, feelings and behaviour, and how it can affect adversely our physical health and well-being. We learn how to monitor our thinking, and how to trust the messages our body sends us. We look at the topic of change in detail, because today's corporate climate is highly unpredictable – once we get a grasp of what happens during the process of change, we are better able to cope with any upheavals.

When we understand how stress affects us, we can start looking for solutions. Chapter 3 is packed with tried-and-tested suggestions as to how we can help relieve stress and improve our well-being, both physically and mentally. We learn about the importance of controlling our breathing, of taking the right kind of exercise, of eating healthy food, and of getting a good night's sleep. We also find out how to release mental stress through thinking more positively, rebalancing our work and home lives and finding new goals and dreams, to form a comprehensive stress-busting strategy.

Chapter 4 is dedicated to offering specific answers to specific problems, covering how to deal with a comprehensive cross-section of the most common problems managers face in the workplace. Topics covered range from decision-making, assertiveness and communication to time management, delegation and harassment. We are given an array of proven methods with which to tackle them, which include recommended forms of exercise or relaxation presented in symbols in the margin (only the symbols depicted in full-strength colour apply to that particular problem). A detailed key to the symbols can be found in the box below.

Finally, when we find ourselves in difficult situations, we sometimes need a quick-fix to instantly release tension. Chapter 5 is full of exercises that do just that, to help us stay calm and focused.

A GUIDE TO SYMBOLS (CHAPTER 4)

The symbols in the margins suggest the most appropriate forms of exercise and relaxation that will support our well-being according to the type of problems we are facing.

 1. **Release Frustration**: *strenuous exercise, such as squash, tennis, hitting a punchbag in the gym and so on.*

 2. **Focus Inward**: *gentle exercise, such as yoga, t'ai chi, qi gong, stretching and so on.*

 3. **Meditate Mindfully**: *calming meditation performed mindfully, alone or in a class.*

 4. **Relax Through Touch**: *professional touch therapy, such as massage, shiatsu, reiki and so on.*

 5. **Improve Fitness**: *cardiovascular or aerobic exercise, such as running, cycling, swimming and so on.*

WHAT'S HAPPENING TO US?

In the twenty-first century the working world is a challenging place in which to be: the Internet has transformed the speed of communication so that we often struggle to keep up with all the emails and information we receive; and we have to live with the fact that the ethos of "jobs for life" has been completely discarded and companies are now more ruthless than ever in "downsizing" if this will help them keep ahead of the competition.

However, every single human being who is part of this hectic, insecure working world is made of flesh and blood. We evolved to deal with a very different world. Certainly primitive humans must have had desperate, terrifying and competitive moments to cope with; but equally they must have enjoyed some tranquil times, too. Today, our lives often seem relentlessly stressful.

In this chapter we take an overview of the impact that stress has on us in our workplace; we explore how it affects both body and mind; and we learn about the most common stressors and how we can assess what causes us the most stress at work.

STRESS: AN OCCUPATIONAL HAZARD?

"Stress" has acquired a bad reputation. Originally, the term was used mainly by architects and engineers: a measurement of pressure exerted on to materials, such as metal, so that designers of buildings and bridges could calculate whether structures were safe or likely to collapse. Then, in the last few decades of the twentieth century, the notion of "stress" came to be applied to the negative pressures that humans experience in life, particularly in the work environment.

In fact, a certain amount of stress can create excitement and challenge. Have you ever been part of a talented, committed team that has a complex task to perform within an exceptionally tight deadline? As the team's anxiety levels start to rise, everyone pulls out all the stops, and a kind of anxious

THE YERKES–DODSON LAW

The Yerkes–Dodson Law was first observed by psychologists Robert M.
Yerkes and John D. Dodson in 1908 when they pioneered the "inverted
'U' model" of pressure measured against productivity. The model
shows us that when our stress levels exceed a certain threshold and
reach the level of overload, and when this high level is sustained over
a period of time, our performance diminishes, we lose efficiency and
our health is dramatically undermined.

The model also reveals that both high and (perhaps surprisingly) low
levels of pressure (or stress) result in low performance. However, at
an intermediate level, there is optimum stimulation and positive effort
– and our productivity is at its peak.

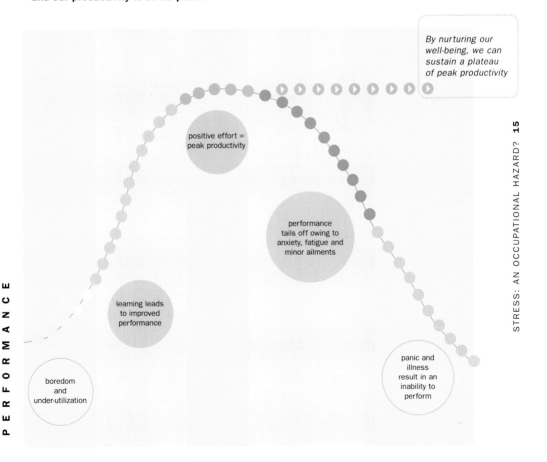

*By nurturing our
well-being, we can
sustain a plateau
of peak productivity*

positive effort =
peak productivity

performance
tails off owing to
anxiety, fatigue and
minor ailments

learning leads
to improved
performance

boredom
and
under-utilization

panic and
illness
result in an
inability to
perform

P E R F O R M A N C E

P R E S S U R E   /   S T R E S S

exhilaration takes over. The work gathers momentum and the results are spectacular. Afterward, everyone falls flat on their backs and asks "However did we do that?" The achievement is remembered with real pride, tempered with relief that it's over.

So, short-term stress can be exhilarating and it can lift our performance to an extraordinary level. When, then, does stress become a problem? Interestingly enough, it is not only when we are overloaded – too little stress can be stress-

ful, too! This sounds contradictory; however, when a person is severely under-employed they become bored and frustrated – conditions that also create stress. I remember a bright college student talking gloomily about her grindingly boring vacation job: "I could do it with my eyes closed – in fact, some of the time I do do it with my eyes closed … ."

Stress, then, only assumes its nefarious character when it becomes relentless and permanent. If people are temporarily overloaded and they pull out all the stops, they relieve themselves of the pressure in the short-term. However, to beat stress in the longer term they need to put into practice the stress management techniques we discuss later on in this book.

THE IMPACT OF STRESS
ON THE WORKING WORLD

In the working world today, competition is relentless, demanding constant innovation and increases in productivity. Company success is driven by the need to stay ahead of rivals. Grim-faced senior managers, themselves stressed and permanently tired, use terse phrases such as "If you can't stand the heat, get out of the kitchen – that's the way it is." This is said even in companies who proudly make statements such as "Our people are our most valuable asset!" In the corporate world today, sadly, most employees operate at overload level. Let's take a look at some statistics.

- *People in the United States now have the longest working hours in the industrialized world.*

- *A huge 78 per cent of US workers describe their jobs as stressful, and 50 per cent say they experience high stress every day.*

- *The US National Safety Council estimates that 1 million employees are absent on an average work day because of stress-related problems.*

- *United States' businesses spend well over $1 billion every year on medical bills for their stressed employees.*

- *A quarter of all employees in the United States describe their job as the number one stressor in their lives.*

- *In the United States, employees aged between 25 and 44 have a 25 per cent chance of being so stressed that their daily productivity levels fall by one third.*

This is a sorry picture. One person off sick with stress creates ripples of consequences like a pebble thrown in a pond. Life is hard for the stressed person, and the impact inevitably spreads to family, friends, colleagues and clients. People can't realize their full potential when they're exhausted and unwell. When companies recognize that people really are their most valuable commodity, their only rational response can be to support their employees in managing stress positively.

THE IMPORTANCE OF
THE BODY–MIND CONNECTION

In the West we often think of our mind as something separate from our body. We reason that our mind is there to process information and to solve problems, while our body allows us to carry out actions physically. In this scenario, healthy mental functioning isn't facilitated by attending to the body; and the well-being of the body isn't influenced by attending to the mind. However, body and mind are not independent. The fact is, body and mind are inextricably linked and they support one another's well-being. Vast amounts of research-based evidence show indisputably how mind and body affect each other, even at the chemical and cellular levels. This knowledge is hugely empowering. For

example, many people have discovered how performing a simple visualization exercise can help them relax before they undergo a stressful experience, such as a job interview.

The workplace today can feel like a permanent treadmill. We can have our "red-alert" button pushed many times a day, so that our bodies are kept in a continuous state of "fight or flight". This can, and does, lead us to develop debilitating stress, mental distress and illness.

We know that corporate life is stressful. At first, it might seem that the only way to reduce this stress is to "downshift"; but with an understanding of the body–mind connection, there is another option – we can change the way we respond to a stressful environment.

I have spoken to thousands of people in corporate life about the body-mind connection. Most had heard of the concept but hadn't fully grasped the extraordinarily positive implications of harnessing that link. Many of them had regarded their brains as "the important part", while their bodies were simply what they lived in – sometimes quite a long-suffering and neglected abode! Learning specific ways in which looking after your physical well-being can improve your cognitive function and problem-solving abilities, or discovering how certain mental exercises can lower your blood pressure, improve your sleep and boost your immune function, can be a revelation. The body-mind connection can also transform your physical well-being and your ability to live your life to the full. A company doctor once said to me "Why wasn't I taught this stuff when I was training?"

We will be exploring the body-mind connection throughout this book. You will find tried-and-tested exercises to enable you to learn, one step at a time, powerful ways to understand and change the way you relate to stress. As you develop skilful management of your mental and physical energy, you will be able to optimize your well-being and help realize your goals.

THE CHEMISTRY OF STRESS

As human beings living busy lives, our minds are kept busy interpreting what is going on around us. Every event that we notice, however tiny or enormous, has to pass through our mental filter; we assess, compare, consider and evaluate thousands of time a day. For example, when we arrive at the office we might think: The boss looks grim today – I wonder why? Or, if we are asked to finish extra work by the end of the day, we might ask ourselves: How will I manage to get everything done and leave on time tonight to watch my son's ballgame?

Every time your mind interprets something as unusual, exciting or alarming, your body is instantly primed for action. This is often called the "fight-or-flight" response, and it's a life-saving function. Think of the sudden epinephrine (adrenaline) rush you experience if you have a near miss in a car, or you hear a strange noise at night.

This "red alert" response has one sole function – to enable your muscles to work very hard and fast, in case you need to escape or do battle. Muscles are fuelled by oxygen and glucose. So your entire physiology changes to make top priority the speedy transportation of these fuels around the body. Your heart rate and blood pressure leap. Anything else going on in the body, such as digestion, slows down or stops. It's a bit like a fire alarm going off in your workplace: everything is put on hold while people leave the building. If there's no fire, people make their way back and normal life resumes. Similarly, when the red alert in your body is over, your parasympathetic nervous system calms everything down again, and life carries on as before.

However, imagine the fire alarm going off every single day – what would this do to the organization within the building? The pace and pressure of life today is such that for many people, that stress response is elicited dozens of times a day, for weeks or months, and the body never has a chance to calm itself down and regain its natural equilibrium.

Your body can cope with this for a time; but eventually, body systems begin to suffer. For example, blood pressure rises, or the immune system loses its ability to fend off invaders, or digestion becomes difficult. During years of lecturing on stress, I have asked thousands of delegates "Is there anyone here who has never once had their guts upset by stress?" The answer is almost no one.

Chronic stress, when your body is in a permanent state of "red alert", can feel, as one delegate put it, "like running along an endless tunnel with no light at the end, and a

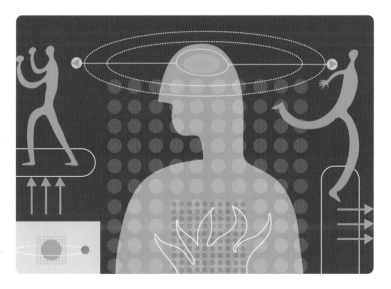

backpack full of rocks on your back. And all you can do is keep running even when you're exhausted." Chronic stress can be ravaging to health; ultimately, it's a killer. Half of all working Americans experience high stress every day. This is no way to live, and it doesn't have to be this way.

what is burnout?

Those who have suffered burnout always recall it with horror. A company director remembers burnout, years later, with a shudder. "I thought I was dying, or going mad," he says. At the time it happened, his wife rang me one morning, very frightened. Her husband was curled in bed in the fetal position and said he couldn't get up and face the day. He had been working flat out for a couple of years; the pace had been relentless and he had driven himself to stay on top of everything. He had not factored self-care into his punishing schedule – there was "no time".

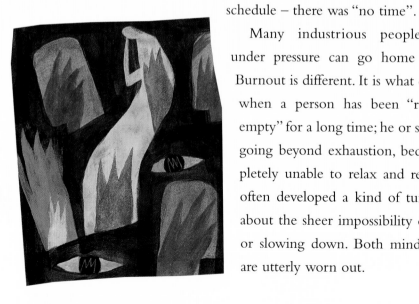

Many industrious people working under pressure can go home exhausted. Burnout is different. It is what can happen when a person has been "running on empty" for a long time; he or she has kept going beyond exhaustion, become completely unable to relax and rest, and has often developed a kind of tunnel vision about the sheer impossibility of stopping or slowing down. Both mind and body are utterly worn out.

One day the person just can't go on. It's a very frightening experience indeed, which, to the person suffering it, can feel as if the whole world is falling apart.

Afterward, serious time out is needed, usually weeks or months; and a complete re-evaluation of life balance is essential. People who have burned out never allow it to happen twice. The sad thing is, it need never happen at all.

regaining equilibrium

There's something amazing that our bodies can do, something we take completely for granted – healing. If we break a leg, do we think "Oh no – I've got to drag around a broken leg for the rest of my life"? Of course not. We know that our body will heal itself to the best of its ability. The same is true when we recover from stress. Once the "red alert" has passed, the process of re-balancing starts: we calm down again, our system operates with optimal efficiency and we feel relaxed, energetic and alert.

Life today triggers the stress response in us constantly. Given that the consequences for our health are dire, can we help our bodies to regain their natural equilibrium? Yes, we can. We can activate the relaxation reponse – a physical state of deep rest – which returns us to that healthy state of equilibrium. I have worked with many business people who now use my techniques to relax and release stress from their bodies and minds every day. As you follow the methods set out in this book, you too will learn how to reap the benefits of improved health, well-being and happiness.

ASSESS YOUR STRESSORS

There are two excellent reasons why you should assess the stressors in your life. The first is so that you become fully aware that something is, in fact, a source of stress (so that you can do something about it). A competent young woman with a bullying boss said to me, "I knew the relationship with him wasn't easy – but it wasn't until he went on holiday that I realized how incredibly tense I'd been in his presence."

The second reason follows on from the first. Once you're clear about what your stressors are, the next questions to ask yourself are: is the source of stress actually internal, that is, rooted in the way I allow something to impact on me? The young woman above was nervous of drawing boundaries with her boss's bullying behaviour, in case she lost her job. Doing a search of other job opportunites and realizing how

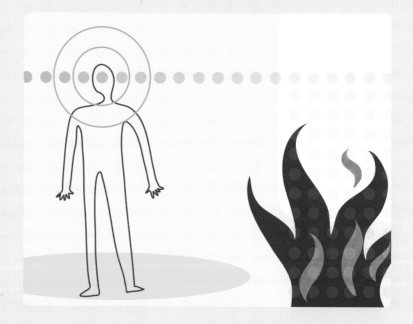

The workplace is a potential minefield of stressors (not forgetting it's also a source of challenge, interest, fulfilment, sociability, excitement and income!). Studies show which aspects of work life are likely to cause the greatest day-to-day pressure on people. They are:

- *constant interruptions*
- *time pressures and deadlines*
- *poor internal communications*
- *lack of support*
- *poor senior management*
- *too many internal meetings*
- *office politics*
- *handling change*
- *securing the right information*
- *keeping up with emails*

employable she was, made it possible for her to speak out assertively and improve the relationship.

If you do not think that the source of stress is internal, ask yourself if this stressor is an external one that you can change by taking action at work, such as refusing to accept unrealistic deadlines, creating new communication systems, leaving work on time, seeking training in new technology and so on. Analyze what specific strategies would raise your stress threshold and your overall well-being at work and then try to implement them.

Sometimes the stressor is external and, although it affects your performance at work, it originates outside the workplace. Take the case of a senior manager in his thirties – an energetic, focused man who was happily married and loved his job. He came to see me because he'd recently found to his amazement that his blood pressure was raised, and he had developed migraines. This didn't fit with his picture of himself as a healthy, ambitious go-getter. We explored possible causes together, looking not only at his work situation, but also at his life as a whole. During the previous eighteen months he had got married, worked for six months in the Far East, returned home again and been promoted – which necessitated moving house and taking on a bigger mortgage – *and* he'd become a father for the first time … you get the picture. Basically, there had been so many changes in his life in a short period of time that his health had suffered. (Research has shown that if life changes come too close together, or if they are big changes, such as getting divorced or the death of someone close, statistically people are likely to become ill in subsequent months.)

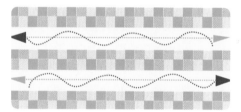

Relationships at home are another aspect we need to consider when we're auditing sources of stress. If things at home are going well, it's our haven – the place where we can relax and be ourselves; it's where love is. But, if our home life is strained, and a source of unhappiness, this will inevitably have a knock-on, adverse effect on our work performance.

Perhaps the worst scenario of all is when you have a stressful work life *and* your home life is also going badly. This is when you must act swiftly – an urgent re-assessment of your life is needed. Standing back and assessing your stressors will provide you with the broader picture, opening the way for insights into how you can make the necessary changes to bring both your career and your personal life back on track.

WORK SOLUTION 1

A Personal Stress Audit

Understanding which aspects of your life create stress is the first step to managing it, both at work and at home. Your Personal Stress Audit will take time and privacy. It should not be rushed.

1. Sit somewhere quiet and undisturbed. Taking a pen and paper, write a brief list of any significant events that have happened in your life over the last two years.

2. Now divide your life into categories, such as Work, Relationship, Children, Family, Friends, Finances and so on. Write them down as headings.

3. Taking each category in turn, note down anything that causes tension or anxiety, or makes you feel sad or angry, taking care not to judge or censor yourself. Keep going until you feel that there's nothing more to add.

4. Looking at each category, are there any common themes that stand out? Are there any areas of stress linking one category to another, for example long working hours causing unhappiness in your relationship? If so, draw a line connecting them to each other. Then, circle anything you know you must change, and asterisk anything else that you feel should be a priority.

5. Now create a strategy to reduce stress. There should be no woolly generalizations; it should contain very specific, achievable steps toward the goal of eliminating each stressor. For example, if you want to cut back long working hours, steps you could take might include: discussing the situation with your boss; delegating more; minimizing time spent in meetings, and so on. Be determined to move forward – taking these steps will make you feel back in control.

chapter 2

WHAT'S HAPPENING TO ME?

Western culture has always separated the mind from the body. But the work of American neuroscientist Professor Candace Pert, among others, has shown how intimately linked they really are. For example, the thought: "My director wants to see me tomorrow to discuss the regional sales figures; he isn't going to be pleased that they're down on last month's", leads to a feeling of anxiety that produces a predictable chemical response in the body. So what and how we think has a direct effect on us physically.

In this chapter, we explore in depth how stress can affect you personally, how it can influence your thinking, feelings and behaviour, and how it can undermine your physical health and well-being. You learn how to observe and analyze your thinking rather than be controlled by it, and how to treat your body as a wonderful and trustworthy resource. Because the working world is always in a state of flux, with mergers, downsizing and takeovers becoming ever more common, we also look closely at the impact of change so that you understand its process and find the best ways to get through difficult times.

YOUR BODY'S MESSAGES

Most of us carry tension in our bodies all the time. It's so familiar that it "feels like home". I remember giving a massage to one client who lay on my couch rigid with chronic tension, saying "This is so great – I haven't felt this relaxed in ages." She meant it; but she had no body-memory of what deep relaxation really feels like. (Two years of regular treatments later, her capacity to relax was transformed, and she almost had to be peeled off the couch.)

When we are habitually mentally stressed, there is always a reflection of that stress in our bodies: tense shoulders and neck, headaches, aching back, upset stomach, eczema, insomnia – the list is long. One thirty-year-old man, recently promoted, felt things were going pretty well except for his stomach. I asked him what he meant; "Well," he said with some embarrassment, "it's ridiculous. I have an upset stomach all the time – I have to know where the nearest men's room is or I get really anxious." I've noticed time and again that hard-working, dedicated people regard physical ailments as "My body's letting me down – it's a real nuisance." They will do their best to keep motoring through relentless hours, trying to ignore the physical discomfort.

This is an attitude based on ignorance, which is not only disrespectful to your miraculous and hard-working body, it's potentially dangerous to your

CONDITIONS THAT
CAN BE STRESS-RELATED

Immune System:
reduced resistance to infections, allergies;
herpes outbreaks

Respiratory System:
asthma, sore throats, sinus problems,
tendency to bronchitis or chest infections

Nervous System:
fatigue, trembling, excessive sweating,
dizziness, restlessness, migraines, insomnia

Digestive System:
mouth ulcers, stomach ulcers, heartburn, indigestion,
nausea, diarrhea, constipation,
hemorrhoids, flatulence,
belching, colitis, irritable bowel syndrome

Cardiovascular System:
tachycardia (over-rapid heartbeat),
palpitations, high blood pressure,
chest pain, heart attacks,
dizziness, fainting

Musculoskeletal System:
stiffness, shoulder and neck pain,
backache, headaches

Hormonal System:
PMT, irregular menstruation,
constant "adrenal charge", low libido

Skin and Hair:
eczema, urticaria, psoriasis,
dermatitis, alopecia (non-hereditary hair-loss)

health. Sadly, people who are over-attached to this attitude can even pay with their lives – that's how seriously you should take this.

Your body is potentially your most trustworthy messenger. Trust it, and begin to listen to what it's telling you. Ignoring your body's messages is like receiving important documents through the mail and throwing away the envelopes unopened. The man with the "unreliable" stomach realized how anxious he'd been feeling. There was an aspect of his new job that he didn't fully understand; he hadn't wanted to ask his manager for fear of looking foolish and incompetent, and also he was working such long hours that he was tense with fatigue, which in turn had an adverse impact on his home life. Eventually, he found a way of speaking to his manager, which resolved much of the anxiety, and he made a decision to leave work on time three days a week – a positive outcome that came from listening to his body.

People have their own "pattern" of minor ills that surface under pressure; for example, they might get one or more symptoms, such as headaches, digestive problems, backache, insomnia or eczema. Make a note of your own pattern of physical reactions to stress. Once you learn to recognize the signs, you will be in a position to manage your stress levels before your health is undermined. Try Work Solution 2, Plotting Your Body Map (opposite), to help raise your awareness of your body.

WORK SOLUTION 2

Plotting Your Body Map

**The focus of this exercise is to make you more aware of your minor ailments –
what they are, when you tend to have them, and why – so that you can
create better stress-release strategies and make them part of your life.**

1. Draw a large, simple outline of your body. This is your body map.

2. Now sit quietly for a few minutes with your eyes closed. Take your whole
attention into your body and analyze how it has felt to live in it lately. Begin at the
top of your head. Scan every part, asking yourself "Do I ever have problems with
this part of me?" Without judgment, mentally log even the little things: eye strain,
a tight neck, backache, an upset stomach, whatever it may be.

3. When you have finished, open your eyes. Take a pen and on your body map
circle the parts of your body where you habitually experience problems. Note any
other relevant information, such as the frequency and intensity of the problem,
outside the outline.

4. Over the next four weeks, monitor your body carefully and make a note of when
these minor ills arise. Analyze the stress-link: what's been going on in your life?

5. Ask yourself: what are these ailments telling me? What does my body need me
to do? Then vow to make one specific change to the way in which you handle your
life. For example, you might decide that instead of heading straight for the bar after
a hard day, you'll take a massage or spend 10 minutes working through Work
Solution 5, Focusing On Your Breath (see p.57), and so on – whatever works best
for you. The important thing is that you make the change and stick with it.

YOUR SPLIT PERSONALITY

I know a delightful, responsible and hard-working executive with a generous nature, who handles interpersonal relationships at work with care and skill. He is inclined to take on too much and finds it hard to say no, so he can become overloaded. He is a high-energy man who thrives under pressure; but occasionally he has what he calls "the last straw scenario" – someone gives him yet more work, and he suddenly "loses it". Files are slapped down on desks. Doors are slammed. His workmates suddenly find that their thoughtful, sunny-natured colleague has become a growling, surly monster. Afterward, he feels very bad and castigates himself for hurting others' feelings.

This is what I call the "Jekyll and Hyde" effect of prolonged pressure. For some people, there's no sudden going off the deep end; it may be a gradual realization that the work they love has become a burden. They no longer care the way they used to, all they want is to walk away from it. Others, who used to love life, wake in the morning with a sense of "Oh no! I've got another day to get through, somehow."

One talented young woman who was making her way up the career ladder paid no attention to managing her stress well, she thought it simply "went with the territory" of corporate life and tried to ignore it. She began to dread and even hate her work – which previously she had loved. She would

WORK SOLUTION 3

Assessing Your "Jekyll and Hyde"

Our usual ways of behaving and feeling can change radically when we are under prolonged pressure. Use this three-pronged Work Solution to identify your own stress patterns of behaviour – it provides you with another excellent way of monitoring your well-being (along with Work Solution 2, Plotting Your Body Map). Then, the moment you notice that you're heading into "Hyde" mode, you can re-evaluate your behaviour, before it is too late.

1. Sit somewhere quiet with a pen and some paper. Take your attention into yourself. Begin by closing your eyes and taking some slow, deep breaths, in and out, for a couple of minutes. Now let yourself think about stressful times from the past, exploring those times as a spectator. How did your attitude to work change when you were under pressure? Did you perhaps switch off and stop caring, or did you become more perfectionist? Did you want to walk out of the job? Consider, too, how your behaviour toward others changed – did you become irritable or intolerant? Did you stop trusting others to do their job? and so on. Describe the changes you noticed – you can use the list on p.37 to help you.

2. Ask friends and trusted colleagues how they know when you are stressed. Tell them that they should be honest. Reassure them that the aim is for them to help you and that you won't be offended or upset by their answers. Often others will say the things you have noticed yourself, but sometimes they'll spot something you weren't aware of.

3. Create a brief personal checklist of your Hyde behaviour. Over a set period of, say, two weeks, run through it every evening to see whether you have behaved in any of your habitual, stressed-out ways. If the answer is yes, look for the trigger, and how you can resolve it, or else how you can release the stress from your body.

wake in the night with a sense of panic. "I tried to do it all myself," she told me ruefully. "I couldn't delegate anymore – I had to keep checking my team's work, changing what they'd done. I thought if I, personally, didn't keep all the balls in the air, the results wouldn't be good enough." You can imagine the effect on the motivation of her team.

When I talk through the Jekyll and Hyde effect with a group of managers and ask them to identify how they change under prolonged pressure, you wouldn't believe how animated the discussion becomes. They are well aware of the ways in which their behaviour deteriorates. Many admit that when they have a bad, frustrating day at work, they are polite all day long, then go home and take it out on their partner or kids. Others describe how they overdose on junk food, or how they become distant and don't want to talk to anyone.

Many people are aware that the more stressed they become, the tighter the grip they try to keep at work. They become perfectionist about everything. "Good enough" is just *not* good enough. They work longer and longer hours, and they become exhausted and rigid with tension.

Feeling tearful at work is something else that many pressurized people experience. Stressed women dread it because they want to seem strong. But don't think that stressed men never feel tearful too – they do. As one competent, energetic and highly stressed man said: "When you get a lump in your throat, you think, 'Absolutely the last thing in the world I'm going to do is burst into tears' – so you've just got to get out of the room and pull yourself together."

These changes in our normal attitudes or behaviour are important. We need to notice they're happening because they're telling us something vital. The message is: stress is forcing you to become somebody you're not and you must take charge again before things get worse.

HOW STRESS CAN AFFECT OUR ATTITUDE AND BEHAVIOUR

Here are some of the most common changes in attitudes and behaviour that people experience when they are under great pressure. Which ones apply to you?

- being irritable and snappy with colleagues
- coping at work but taking it out on loved ones at home
- sudden explosive temper although you're usually a calm person
- becoming perfectionist – "good enough" just won't do
- avoiding challenging tasks – doing small, unimportant things instead
- finding multi-tasking hard – having a pressing wish to have a single focus
- becoming distant and avoiding contact with workmates
- becoming hypersensitive to criticism
- trying to do everything yourself
- feeling panicky
- feeling tearful
- relying on alcohol
- overdosing on junk food, chocolate or coffee
- wanting to walk away from your work, when you used to enjoy it
- working longer hours without feeling you're getting anywhere
- going over and over things relentlessly in your mind
- waking in the night with a head full of work

BUILDING YOUR OWN TIMB BOMB

Do you find that, once or twice a year, you begin to feel seriously overworked? Do your energy levels dive; does paperwork pile up; and you have no time for relaxation, let alone fun? And a couple of weeks later, do you feel really under the weather? If so, you are not alone. Many generally healthy, energetic people have these significant dips in well-being.

It nearly always starts with some genuinely stressful episode – say, a frustrating project that doesn't go well, or anxiety about an impossibly tight deadline. Unless we are skilled in managing stress, we find ourselves dwelling on the problem night and day. Our agitated mind takes over and keeps the body bathed in stress hormones almost continuously – creating our own well-being time bomb.

When we're on "red alert" for weeks or months, life starts to go insidiously out of balance. We stop sleeping well, which drastically affects our energy levels. Fatigue dulls our creativity, we lose flexibility in our thinking and decision-making capability. We realize we're swamped and there's no respite.

We know things aren't right – but do we stop, take stock, and create an effective stress strategy? No. We react by working even harder and longer. We say "I'll take a break when things are a bit easier." We snatch fast food along the way, and keep ourselves going on coffee. Relationships at work suffer. Our home life is neglected: we arrive back late every night, exhausted, and our capacity to relax and have fun disappears, along with our libido. You get the picture – life has become a struggle.

How do we let this happen? Because we do let it happen. Most of us grow up wanting to do our best, which is a healthy, motivating philosophy. However, sometimes we go one step further, and think we are only worthwhile poeple if we're doing our best. And how can you be certain that you're doing your best? Well, you must be – look how exhausted you are! This kind of circular thinking needs to be rooted out.

We each generate both physical and mental energy. Imagine that you have an energy bank account, that you run along the same lines as a money bank account. You make deposits when you balance your workload and your well-being, but have to make withdrawals to sustain you when the balance gets out of kilter. In times of stress, it is easy to find yourself falling into the red, so try to monitor your energy bank-balance wisely, with care and compassion for yourself. Next time you feel yourself becoming stressed or overworked and your energy levels start to plummet, don't just ignore the signs and try to work even harder. Instead, take appropriate action before the situation builds up into a time bomb (see p.33 for how to increase your awareness of what is going on in your body). This will help you notice a downward stress trend *before* it undermines you. There is no reason why your well-being has to yo-yo up and down – with a little effort it is possible to maintain high energy levels and a grounded, stress-proof life *all the time*.

HOW YOUR THINKING CAN
UNDERMINE YOU

Imagine that, when you were peacefully asleep in your bed last night, a crazed axe murderer had come creeping into the room. Would you have been stressed by that? No, not in the least. Remember, you were asleep. Of course, if you'd woken up it would have been a totally different story.

Your mind acts as a filter between you and the world. Once you're awake, your brain analyzes the situation as: "Person with an axe – creeping – not good news." This is how your mind constantly interprets what's going on in your world and what it means for you.

Now consider a scenario suggested by the well-known mind-body-spirit guru, Dr Deepak Chopra. One day, you're walking along a path in the jungle. You're calm, alert, fascinated by the scents and sounds of this wild place. You turn a corner – and there, ahead of you on the path, is a giant, fully-grown cobra. How would you react?

Most of us would instantly freeze into the fear response – our minds would tell us "DANGER"; our bodies would respond with a rush of epinephrine (adrenaline) and our sole focus would be to escape to safety. However, that's not the only possible reponse, not even the only rational one. What if you were a snake expert? In that case, coming upon this magnificent snake might produce an immediate thought, such as "Wow! Look at this beautiful creature! How can I photograph it safely?" Another possibility is that you are a Hindu, and your mind interprets the snake as a manifestation of the god Shiva. While you would still wish to keep a safe distance from the cobra, your response might be a reverential one. The difference between the first reaction cited and the two that follow is that the first one is totally negative, provoking nothing but fear, whereas the other two reactions both contain a positive element.

So for the walker in the jungle, there are at least three potential mindsets, one of which is highly stressful, the other two much less so – and each of them is self-created.

The workplace can be very like the jungle at times! Every workday holds situations which our minds interpret as good, bad, exciting, worrying and so on. Take the case of the author-itative senior executive, who was in his forties and had been

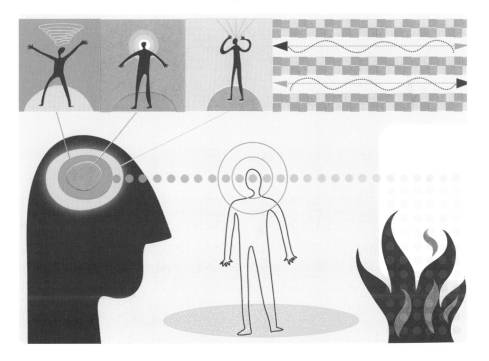

brought up with a strong work ethic and respect for his elders. One Friday, the chairman of the company, an older man, unusually summoned him to a meeting the following Monday. You wouldn't believe the fear this created – it was his very own "business cobra". This competent man went over and over his recent performance. Feeling undermined, he began painting the worst-case scenario: "If I'm fired, what will I do?" After a wretched weekend, Monday came – and the meeting was full of praise, and appreciation. He was even offered a directorship. "I just can't believe how I put myself through such hell for nothing!" he groaned afterward.

We all have thinking habits and it is easy to create thought patterns that are negative and self-destructive. Some of us go over and over things, revisiting stressful memories in our minds, and re-stimulating the "red alert" stress response in our body.

So how can you break this vicious cycle? You can start by getting to know your own thinking habits and identifying how you create stress for yourself (see Work Solution, opposite). Then, you can begin changing the negative aspects. Lay stressful memories to rest – they are in the past. Instead, concentrate on the present and the future. Whenever you find yourself reacting with fear or panic, stop, take a deep breath and look for the positive aspects of the situation. Ask yourself: what can I learn from this? Each time you can focus on the positive in a stressful business situation you are overwriting negative thought patterns, and becoming more confident, more composed and, ultimately, more successful.

WORK SOLUTION 4

Watching the Movie of Your Mind

This Work Solution provides a direct route to a better understanding of your thinking habits. You will discover the kinds of situations that habitually cause you to worry, or feel angry or upset. Becoming more aware of your "trigger" situations helps you to release the grip of old response patterns, and to think in a more constructive way.

1. Sit somewhere comfortable where you won't be disturbed. Close your eyes, take a deep breath and release it slowly. Now conduct a "self-awareness audit", starting with the body. Notice how you feel. For example, which parts of your body feel tense? Don't try to change anything, simply examine yourself as objectively as you can.

2. Now take your attention to your thoughts. Imagine that you can project those thoughts onto an empty movie screen in your mind. As each one comes up, mentally label it to fit in with one of the following three categories:
   - *Past (a thought about something that actually happened)*
   - *Present (a thought about the here and now – usually a message from your senses, such as a feeling of aching shoulders, the smell of coffee, or the sound of traffic, and so on)*
   - *Future (a thought about something that hasn't happened yet)*

3. Once you have labelled each thought, let it fade away. Project your thoughts in this way for 2 or 3 minutes. Then, consider your thinking habits. Do you worry mostly about the past? Or do you mainly speculate about the future? Does a pattern emerge?

4. Spend a few moments in quiet contemplation of the question "Who is it who thinks these thoughts?" Don't struggle for an answer, simply let the question float in your mind. When you feel ready, gently bring your attention back to the present.

KNOWING WHERE YOU ARE WHEN YOU DON'T KNOW WHERE YOU ARE

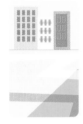

Every one of us needs to develop an understanding of what happens to us in times of uncertainty, and how to work with the situation. There's a common acceptance that today's workplace is much more unpredictable than ever before: mergers, downsizing, dramatic corporate collapses and takeovers are hugely publicized. There's widespread anxiety about the disintegration of old certainties, and a sense of old order heading for new disorder.

Have you noticed how many safeguards we have in everyday life, designed to minimize the shock of change or uncertainty? For example, rationally we know that a huge number of cars are involved in accidents every single day; and as driving a car is such an integral part of ordinary life, we try to prepare for any mishaps by holding insurance. In the business world, risk analysis helps us to decide whether a risk is acceptable. We create comforting, rationally-based frameworks to contain risky, unpredictable situations.

The business world is full of energetic, intelligent and focused people who love a challenge. Success-orientated people are normally at their most relaxed (and therefore their most productive) when their path to success is clear. But as uncertainty is increasingly present in corporate life, maybe a new skill is now needed: the ability to allow yourself to accept periods of uncertainty in a potentially creative way. Of course when things fall into chaos, we try to re-order them. We try to frame uncertainty, make sense of it and find a resolution. Sometimes, though, if we do this prematurely, we choke the evolution of new possibilites.

A time of uncertainty can be a potential hot-bed of new ideas – not new ideas that can be reached via logical thinking, but through novel thinking that flowers only from the seedbed of chaos. And the only way to make space for extraordinary, creative things to bloom, is being willing to tolerate a time of being lost. So success, in this situation, means the day-to-day sustaining of your own willingness to embrace chaos. This is hard. It means accepting that a state of confusion is the way it is right now, staying with that, and having complete faith that the situation will evolve.

UNDERSTANDING THE CHANGE JOURNEY

One thing we can be sure of – life never stands still. Plan as we may for every eventuality, something unexpected often jumps into the picture. Every time we encounter change in our lives, the emotional process we have to go through is similar. I call it the Change Journey. Once you understand the Change Journey map (see opposite), you can navigate your life with greater understanding and become a more effective manager and leader.

The first stage of the Change Journey is shock. Your reaction could be anything from disbelief to speechlessness. When in shock the human brain can't digest information, so if you are given news of a big change – say, that you are to transfer to head up a new department – allow time for the news to sink in. Make an appointment with your boss to discuss the impact or terms of the change the following day.

The second stage of the Change Journey is denial. Our instinct is to prefer to keep things the way they are, which leads to more emotional turmoil. We might feel angry, perhaps sad – even humiliated or guilty. This emotional rollercoaster can't be rushed, it's an organic process. The healthiest solution is to express these feelings. Try releasing your anger by going running or using a punchbag at the gym.

Acceptance comes over time. When your emotions settle, make a conscious decision to let go of the past and welcome in new ideas to open up your thinking. Soon enough you'll find the meaning (and the benefit) in what happened and ultimately you'll be able to integrate the change into your life fully. More often than not the outcome is a happy one – you become wiser, more courageous and more adventurous as a result of the change.

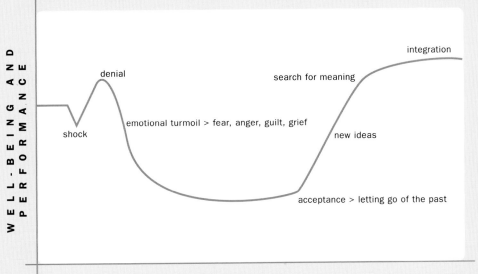

COPING WITH CREEPING CHANGE

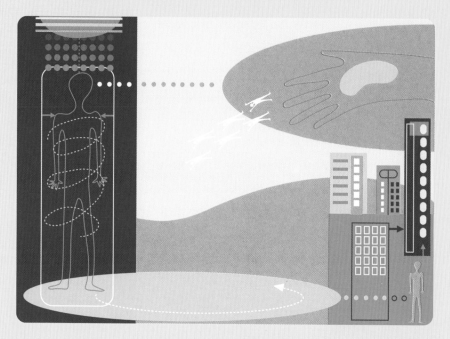

Now that you understand the process your body and mind go through when an unexpected change happens (and how to deal with that process), you need to learn how to deal with creeping change – the kind of change that happens subversively and over time. Sometimes it's this kind of change that can be most stressful – one day we arrive at the office and realize that things are completely different from how they used to be, and we've no recollection of things changing. As managers, we can find this particularly upsetting – after all, aren't managers supposed to be the people with their fingers on the pulse? Shouldn't we have the whole business strategy mapped out in the finest detail?

Even the most successful business people get taken by surprise sometimes. This is especially true in small companies where growth (a good thing when well-managed) leads to subtle shifts in roles and responsibilities, company procedures and perspectives, until suddenly something happens to make us notice the change. Perhaps the new processes work well, or perhaps formal restructuring is needed. Either way, allow yourself to travel the Change Journey and then review the situation. The most important thing now is to put aside your feelings of unease and find your feet.

Where creeping change is just part of the organic process of a growing business, there's little point in trying to work out where and when it happened – change is natural and inevitable. Now is the time to assess where you are and where you are going. Start by looking at your staff. Who does what? Are all the jobs clearly defined (in principle, but most importantly in practice) including your own? Usually creeping change means that people's jobs have grown or shifted, but original responsibilities remain. In some respects this is a good thing (increased productivity), but are you now paying your most senior people to do junior work? Has growth in your department meant that you could do with some additional support? Now look at systems. Are things as efficient as they used to be? Are the channels of communication clear? Ask for your colleagues' feedback – what things frustrate them? What further changes need to take place to help your day-to-day working processes catch up with the company's own evolution? Devise a plan and gain support for it from your team. The more you take control of the situation, the more confident and relaxed you will feel about change.

chapter 3

HOW CAN I HELP MYSELF?

In Chapters 1 and 2 we've looked at ways in which the working world can impact on you physically and mentally. Having reached a new understanding of the interface between you and your workplace means that you're now in a good position to help yourself by taking practical steps to relieve stress and promote well-being.

In this chapter we consider a wide variety of techniques that can help you realize your goals. You learn how to think positively and how to control your breathing; how to take the right kind of exercise; why touch therapy, such as massage is beneficial; how to eat healthily; and how to improve your sleep. We also explore how you can rebalance your life; improve your working environment; rekindle inspiration; and create a climate for change. The many supportive methods described here have all been road-tested by people in corporate life and can help you to create a powerful set of life strategies.

DEFUSE YOUR INNER CRITIC

Many of us have an Inner Critic who is always ready and willing to offer an opinion about us as people, our perform-ance at work and life in general. Strange, isn't it, how the Inner Critic never has anything positive to say?

As we grow up, the parents and teachers whose job it is to help us become responsible adults, guide us through childhood with all manner of instruction, expectation, encouragement, criticism and praise. Along the way we absorb their advice, and we internalize it as messages about ourselves as people, the way we should be in the world and what the world is like.

This is a natural process and helps shape us as people, mostly in a positive way. Quite often, though, along with all the good and helpful messages, we internalize one or two "inner voices" from our childhood that are negative and unhelpful. Working with managers, I've found it very poignant that many of these energetic, focused people have Inner Critic voices that are harsh and say unhelpful things such as: "You're only a worthwhile person if you're success-ful", or "No-one will forgive you if you make a mistake."

These Inner Critics tend to operate on the edge of our consciousness, subtly undermining us, no matter how suc-cessfully we operate in the real world. They sabotage confi-dence, self-esteem and your sense of yourself as a strong, competent person. When you become aware of a shadowy Inner Critic operating within, it's valuable to put it under the spotlight. Ask yourself, how is it undermining you or making you needlessly anxious? Write down the message it seems to be sending you – for example, it might say "You may think that presentation went well, but don't kid yourself – they were probably thinking 'What a loser'."

Then send in the cavalry, in the form of a new, positive voice – your Inner Coach – which you need to develop consciously in yourself. People with vocal Inner Critics sometimes find it hard at first to formulate the positive way in which an Inner Coach would address them. The trick is to copy how you yourself would speak to a good and trusted friend – you would be honest, loving, realistic, encouraging and firmly on their side; and you would confirm and celebrate everything of value, making helpful suggestions.

So when the Inner Critic starts pecking away at your self-esteem, your Inner Coach should say "Rubbish, of course the presentation went well. You were well prepared, you delivered it in a relaxed, fluent way. Did you notice how intently they listened? And how focused their questions were? It was a very good presentation – feel proud of yourself." Your Inner Coach can also let you know in a matter-of-fact, objective way, how you could improve; for example by following the above praise with "Next time, you could make the presentation even better by spreading your eye contact around the room so that you involve the whole audience."

Practise developing the positive voice of your own Inner Coach and, over time, the negative voice of your Inner Critic will gradually fade away.

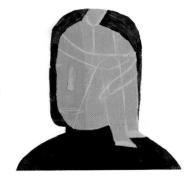

BREATHE TRANQUILLY

As you begin reading this page, without changing a thing, notice how you're breathing. The odds are, your breathing is slight: a gentle, barely discernible movement of air in and out of the top of your chest. It's the way most people breathe for much of their working day. While it obviously keeps you alive and functioning, this is not the best way to breathe. Your breath is one of the ways you nourish your body and expel waste gases so that your metabolism can function efficiently; if you only breathe shallowly, both your body and your thinking are more sluggish and less alive than they could be.

We take breathing for granted. People can live without food for weeks, and without water for days; but without breathing in air we would be dead in minutes. The fact is, breathing not only keeps you alive; it is also, as we will see, one of the best ways of releasing stress from body and mind.

Merely taking a moment to fill your lungs and breathe deeply can calm you when you find yourself pressurized.

Start by consciously taking a deep breath, and note exactly how your ribs and shoulders move. I've noticed time after time that if I ask a group of people to take a deep breath, most will take a great gulp of air which lifts the ribs, chest, and sometimes the shoulders upward. In actual fact, this is a limited way to breathe.

A friend who is a top-level sports coach relates how he didn't learn to breathe well until he reached his mid-twenties, after already spending some years as a professional footballer. He had always done the chest-lifting breath. Changing the way he breathed was hard at first; but learning to expand his breathing not only extended him as a sportsman, but also helped him to feel more grounded physically.

So, take a few moments now to explore breathing differently. Sit, or stand, or lie flat and try this: lay your hands lightly on your belly, relax your stomach and midriff, and take a long, slow breath deep into your body. Forget your chest: imagine that the in-breath is slowly blowing up a balloon in your belly. You will feel your hands move slightly outward. Then release the breath totally; your hands will move in toward each other. You may find that after a few of these deep, focused breaths, your body suddenly does a spontaneous deep breath all on its own, bringing with it a sense of release and relaxation.

If you notice yourself breathing shallowly at work, try re-charging yourself or releasing tension with a replenishing

breath right down into your belly. It's possible to do this quite discreetly.

Meditation using the breath provides an incredibly powerful form of stress release. If you've never tried meditation, or decided it's not for you, think again. There is nothing other-worldly about it, and anyone can do it. In many cultures, it is part of a person's spiritual practice; but for thousands of Western managers and leaders, it's an indispensable tool for building focus and tranquillity in daily life.

Put simply, meditation means sitting quietly and concentrating your attention on one thing totally, such as your breath, a candle flame, a picture or a mantra (a sound or a word). Focusing on your breath for ten minutes may sound easy, but in fact it takes intense concentration. As you put all your awareness into how it feels to breathe, your mind gets really sneaky. Rather than stay focused, it pops in a thought or two. When you realize that your mind has wandered, you need to bring it back to your breath. You may have to re-focus in this way dozens of times at first, but it becomes easier with practice.

The main physiological benefit of meditation is that the heart rate slows and the blood pressure falls. While normally brainwaves follow a fast beta rhythm (13 to 30 cycles per second), and the brain is in an active, left-brain, "doing" mindstate, when we listen to music, walk in the park or meditate, it adopts an alpha rhythm (7 to 13 cycles per second) a relaxed, right-brain, "being" mindstate. In the longer term, daily meditation can lower high blood pressure significantly.

WORK SOLUTION 5

Focusing On Your Breath

This simple meditation is an effective way of releasing the powerful grip that stressful thinking can have on your mind and body. Practise the process for a few minutes every day. It will soon become part of your routine – a special time when you can relax and re-charge your energy.

1. Find somewhere quiet where you won't be disturbed. Sit with your feet on the floor, your hands resting in your lap, and your spine upright, but relaxed. Imagine your vertebrae are like the beads on a necklace, suspended from one end. Close your eyes, or keep them only slightly open – your focus should be inward.

2. Take some deeper breaths to help you settle. Let your breath flow right down to your stomach, then release it.

3. Mentally scan your body. Without trying to change anything, assess which parts feel relaxed and which are tense or uncomfortable.

4. Now focus your awareness on your breath. Notice all the subtle sensations of breathing in and out; how the temperature of the in-breath is different from that of the out-breath; how your ribcage and your diaphragm expand and contract each time you breathe. If distracting thoughts come into your head, simply let them go and gently bring your attention back to your breathing.

5. After about 10 minutes, or when you are ready to finish the meditation, allow your attention to drift back to everyday reality.

GET PHYSICAL

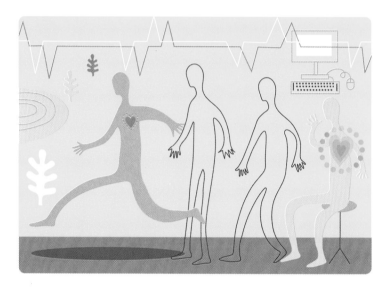

Most of us spend a large amount of our time sitting down – travelling to and from work, hunching over a desk or a computer screen, sitting in meetings, or slumping in front of the television after a draining day. Mentally we are relentlessly active, but physically we often become sedentary, almost without noticing. This is not a good recipe for well-being.

The fact is, a neglected, unfit body undermines our capacity for optimal mental performance, and our physical deterioration begins insidiously. We don't always notice how our mental capability and resilience are also undermined. Remember the dynamic link between mind and body: if you want to develop your full potential, you need to include a commitment to build your physical fitness and health.

Many people who are committed to looking after their bodies go to the gym three times a week, do their regular work-out, then mentally tick the box marked "fitness" – their routine doesn't change. This is better than no exercise at all, but it has its limitations. Your body needs different types of exercise in different circumstances, and the challenge is to recognize your body's needs as they change.

The bedrock of most people's exercise regimes is a cardiovascular or aerobic work-out. There is a good reason for this. One of the ways in which athletes' fitness is measured is by the speed of their recovery time – how rapidly their heart rate returns to normal following the stress of performance. In business life, when you are dealing with stressors on a daily basis, there is no doubt that the impact on your body is less damaging if you are fit. In other words, every time your heart rate is raised in response to, say,

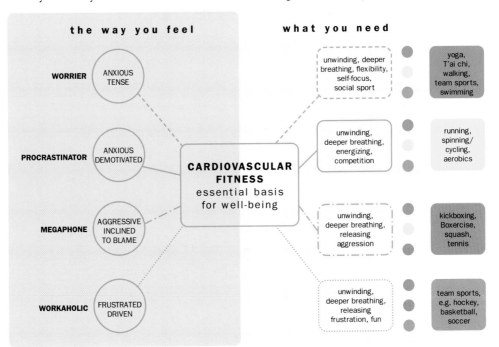

making a presentation or receiving a performance assessment, your recovery time is shorter if you have a fit heart.

Imagine a day full of irritation and exasperation, when everything possible has gone wrong and you feel like punching someone. An effective (and much safer!) way to release this stress would be to hit a punchbag, or to play squash, or to go running – types of exercise through which you can release frustration. And you'd feel so much better afterward.

Now think of a different type of stressful day – one that makes you anxious. Let's say that you are struggling to meet a critical deadline, or that a key member of your team is off sick, or that the monthly figures look grim. In such situations your body needs exercise that will open up your shallow breathing and stretch the tension out of your body. Yoga, Pilates or t'ai chi might fit the bill. Working at your physical flexibility not only gives you poise and helps you avoid injury, but because your body and mind are so intimately linked, when you physically stretch and relax you also relieve built-up mental tension.

If you often find yourself worrying, you might also want to consider doing some strength-building work. Here, again, the body–mind link is significant: if your body is strong, flexible and relaxed, it is virtually impossible to maintain an anxious or fearful mindset for very long.

Try new ways of exercising from time to time, and look for support from good trainers and teachers. As you develop a mindful awareness of your body, it will tell you what exercise you need. Listen to your body and trust it.

WORK SOLUTION 6

Audit Your Exercise Portfolio

Your body needs a range of physical exercise which will fulfil the following five functions: building your cardiovascular fitness; increasing your energy and strength; releasing frustration or anxiety from your body; extending your flexibility; and making you feel good.

1. Sit down with some paper, a pen and your journal. Look back over the last month's entries in the journal and note exactly what exercise (if any) you did, and which of the above functions it fulfilled.

2. Now close your eyes and think about the last month in more detail. Do you remember how you felt at different times? When did you feel good? When were you frustrated, anxious or exhausted? What exercise do you think your body needed, but didn't get during this period? Jot down your answers.

3. Analyze what you have written. Where are the gaps in your exercise portfolio? How can you open up your options to include all five criteria listed above? Don't be afraid to consider taking up new sports or programs.

4. Set aside time in your calendar for at least three exercise sessions per week for the next six weeks. Vow to stick to this schedule, even if you find yourself tempted to give precedence to other, possibly more enjoyable activities, and especially if you feel tempted to work (remember your new exercise program is to help you maximize your professional effectiveness).

5. Finally, imagine yourself as you would like to feel six weeks from now – able to think clearer and focus better; more motivated and productive; and of course, fitter.

DISCOVER THE POWER OF TOUCH

We are born needing touch. Newborn babies need skin contact, and a sense of being held lovingly by adults. This is the basic nurturing that is vital for babies if they are to thrive. A study at the University of Miami's Touch Research Institute showed that when premature babies were gently stroked for 15 minutes three times a day, they gained 47 per cent more weight, were more alert and left hospital six days earlier than other premature babies who did not receive this form of physical attention.

Why is this relevant to us as adults? Because touch still has a powerful role to play in our well-being. It's a sad fact that many people today are deprived of touch. After all, physical contact with another human being, whether it's a hug from a loved one or a massage to relieve tension can create a deep sense of comfort and calm.

The Touch Research Institute has established, many times over, the positive effect of touch on our physiology and our psychological state. Office workers receiving even a short, 15-minute back and shoulder massage through their clothes report increased alertness afterward, and the level of stress hormones in their blood falls.

A Harvard Medical School study reports on two groups of pre-operative patients. On the morning of the operation, a fearful and high-stress time, patients in the control group were visited by the anesthetist, who checked their blood pressure and had a short conversation with them about the operation. However, with a second group of patients, the anesthetist checked their blood pressure and had an identical conversation, but this time while talking with them he sat on the bed and held their hand. The results were unequivocal. On average, patients who had had their hand held needed half the quantity of drugs and left hospital three days earlier than those in the control group. And there are many other studies demonstrating the same principle – that safe touch can release tension and increase well-being in the most amazing way.

Of course for adults, touch is complicated by social taboos and by its association with sexuality. This has created a minefield around touch in the workplace. Those who might instinctively reach out to comfort a stressed colleague by, say, touching them momentarily on the shoulder, first have to check themselves and consider whether such a gesture will be seen as inappropriate.

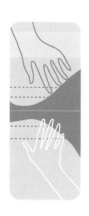

Given that tension is the enemy of vibrant well-being, and that touch is a powerful antidote to tension, what should we do to address the lack of regular, no-strings-attached physical contact in our lives? One solution is to incorporate professional touch into your life by going to a well-trained touch therapy practitioner. There is a whole world of therapies available – different kinds of massage, shiatsu, reflexology and many more – whose sole agenda is to release tension from your body so that your energy can flow.

Whichever touch therapy interests you, make sure that you find a practitioner who is well-qualified, insured and belongs to a professional organization. A first-class practitioner should make you feel completely at ease so that you can allow yourself to relax and open yourself up to the experience. The levels of stress hormones in your blood will then fall, giving your body's natural healing systems a chance to re-establish a healthy equilibrium. In addition, try self-massage – it can be very effective (see Work Solution 7, opposite).

As for timing, you need to have your therapy at least once a month. At times of high stress, increase the frequency of treatment to weekly – don't make the mistake of saying to yourself "I'll just get through this, *then* I'll have a massage and calm down." That would be poor self-management. It would be like putting anti-freeze in your car after the temperature has plummeted. If you find that one type of touch therapy is not to your liking, don't give up – try something else. Once you have been in the right therapy regularly for six months, you will find that you won't ever want to go without it.

WORK SOLUTION 7

Simple Self-Massage

During a pressurized day, we often build up physical tension in our shoulders, neck and face. This simple self-treatment can lift incipient headaches, release tension and banish tiredness.

1. Sit comfortably in a chair, which supports your back. With your right hand, locate the muscle on top of your left shoulder. Your palm should be on the front of your shoulder, fingers and thumb on the back. Squeeze and lift the muscle. Then make circular movements with your fingertips, exploring areas of tension and pressing as deeply as feels good. Repeat with your left hand and right shoulder.

2. Now circle your fingertips on both sides of the vertebrae at the back of your neck, moving outward along the bottom edge of your skull. You may find this easier if you drop your head very slightly backward. Press as deep as feels good.

3. Move your fingertips to the hinges of your jaw. Clench your teeth for a moment so that you feel where the jaw muscles are. Then relax your jaw and press into the muscles, circling with your fingertips.

4. Next, place the pads of your thumbs just underneath the inner edge of your eyebrows. Press here for 10 seconds. Release, then press again for another 10 seconds. Then, starting at the centre of your eyebrows, pinch with your forefinger and thumb along to your temples.

5. Now take your middle fingers just beyond the outer edges of your eye sockets – just below your temples. Massage this area with slow, firm circles for 2 minutes. Finish by taking a slow, deep tension-releasing breath, in and out.

EAT YOURSELF WELL

Just as the quality and type of fuel used in a car influence both the performance and the longevity of the engine (you wouldn't put paraffin in your car), so the quality and type of food you eat influence the health, performance and longevity of your body.

Mental performance is one of the key areas that suffers when you're undernourished (and you can still be undernourished even though you eat plenty, if it's plenty of the wrong things). The symptoms range from impaired cognitive function, chronic fatigue and low-level depression to dozens of undesirable ailments from low sperm motility through to high cholesterol levels and, in chronic cases, serious illness. Many diseases are linked with dietary excess or imbalance.

Your diet has a special significance among the lifestyle factors that influence your well-being – simply because you do have total control over what you put in your mouth. So how do you best eat for well-being? First, think about *when* you eat. The old adage "Breakfast like a king, lunch like a prince and dine like a pauper" is good advice. Make sure you eat breakfast and lunch. Eat lightly in the evening so that your body has digested the food before you go to sleep. Then, think about *how* you eat. Don't eat when you're angry, rushed or distracted. Give the food your whole attention, so your body is prepared to receive nourishment. Savour and enjoy every mouthful – eating is a pleasurable process.

How should you decide *what* to eat? Forget food fads and diets and avoid packaged and processed foods, which tend to be full of salt, sugar and fat. During the Second World War, deaths from heart attacks plummeted in the occupied countries of Western Europe, because foods such as butter, cheese and meat – all high in saturated fat – had become scarce. When these foods became available again after the war, deaths from heart attacks rose.

Our bodies are programmed to thrive on simple, fresh produce that grows in the earth, and a small amount of protein. If you eat a wide variety of organic fruits and vegetables, grains, nuts and seeds, including soya, you'll ensure that your body receives the wide range of nutrients that it needs. If you are not vegetarian, also include in your diet small quantities of organic, free-range meat and delicious health-giving fish.

HYDRATE YOUR BODY

Headaches, sluggish thinking and low energy can mean that you are dehydrated. If you ever notice your lips feeling dry, it means you've been dehydrated for a while. Keep a bottle of water by your desk and make a habit of drinking about eight glasses a day.

Another way to keep yourself well-hydrated is to eat fresh fruit during the day – fruit and vegetables are naturally high in water. Try keeping a bowl of ripe, fresh fruit on your desk, too.

IMPROVE YOUR SLEEP QUALITY

According to the American Academy of Sleep Medicine, on any given night more than 100 million US citizens fail to get a good night's sleep. The "thinking" part of our brain, the frontal cortex, needs sleep to recover from the day. It deals with directing and sustaining our attention, our speech, our memory, and our ability for innovative and flexible thinking – skills needed for effective management. The Loughborough Sleep Research Centre in the UK has found that sleep loss affects us dramatically: our ability to think clearly and communicate well deteriorates; we are more easily distracted; our ability to make flexible decisions and quick, rational judgments is impaired; and we lose the capcity to alter our strategy when situations change. It seems clear, then, that in order to perform at an optimal level at work, we need to sleep well.

The effects of sleep loss are very worrying in situations where exhausted people are taking important (or even life-or-death) decisions – for example, in fast-moving business scenarios, such as mergers; in the construction industry; in military situations; or in hospitals. Lack of sleep can be lethal for drivers, especially for those whose work requires them to drive long distances on monotonous highways.

Human beings are designed to sleep twice in twenty-four hours – a long sleep at night and a nap after lunch. In many countries, an afternoon siesta is an accepted part of the day. Many of us have had the experience of sitting after lunch in a less-than-riveting meeting, and having to fight to keep our eyes open! A ten-minute "power-nap" during your lunch break can prevent this. Or, if you're not a person who can nap, take a walk in the fresh air at lunchtime to wake yourself up, and sip plenty of water when you're back at work.

A good night's sleep begins with the way you spend your evening. Try some of the following guidelines to create a new set of habits and attitudes toward sleep. First, avoid taking work home whenever possible, but if you absolutely *have* to put in some extra hours at home, make sure that you finish at a reasonable time – never, ever, take work to bed. Have a light supper with no caffeinated drinks in the evening and no alcohol in the couple of hours before bed. Keep the last

UNDERSTANDING
YOUR BODY'S NATURAL RHYTHMS

Your body has more than 100 circadian rhythms (unique 24-hour cycles), each of which influences an aspect of the way your body functions, including sleep and wakefulness.

Do you find it hard to get going in the morning? Or are you often sleepy in the afternoon, finding it hard to focus? Overriding this natural rhythm and trying to force yourself to be highly alert at the wrong time of day for you, when your cognitive flexibility, awareness and decision-making ability are on a low, is simply not possible.

Getting to know and respecting your own body clock is fundamental for excellent performance. Monitor your pattern of alertness through each working day for two weeks. The information you learn about your own natural rhythm will help you maximize your effectiveness. You can then plan your day effectively, arranging the important meetings for the time when you know you'll be most alert and energetic.

hour of your evening relaxing, mundane and routine, and, if possible, find time to incorporate a meditation, such as Work Solution 5, Focusing On Your Breath (see p.57). Wait until you feel tired before going to bed.

If you find that you can't get to sleep, try the following: using your shower head, run cold water over your legs and feet for 2 minutes. Dry them and get into bed. Your feet will

soon feel as warm as toast and you should find that you drop off to sleep in no time. Don't ask me why this works, but it usually does!

If you wake up in the night and your mind kicks in to overdrive, take your attention away from your thoughts and concentrate on your breathing. Don't ever lie in bed tossing and turning. If you do, you're only training yourself to believe "Bed is where I toss and turn." Instead, get up and engage in a gentle activity in another room – but don't work, watch TV or go on the Internet. The Loughborough Sleep Research Centre suggests that doing a jigsaw can be very effective. Wait until you feel sleepy before going back to bed.

Sleeplessness or sleeping badly are not in themselves harmful. However, if you find yourself thinking "If only I could sleep better, I wouldn't feel so stressed" – you've got things the wrong way round. Stress and anxiety come first; sleeplessness and sleeping badly are symptoms of stress. So, if you are going through a long phase of poor sleep, you need to address the underlying stress that is causing it. Continue working your way through this book, which is full of techniques and suggestions that you can use to banish stress and realize your full potential.

WORK SOLUTION 8

Create Your Own Haven for Sleep

Part of the process of trying to improve your sleep involves making your bedroom into a haven for sleep – a place of total peace and privacy. This exercise shows you how to plan your sleeping environment for maximum tranquillity, so that the minute you walk in, your body and mind can really start to relax.

1. Take a good look around your bedroom. What is the predominant colour? (We all respond differently to colours, but generally most people find blues and greens the most relaxing.) Consider repainting the room in tranquil tones; or choose a neutral colour for the décor and add bed linen, rugs and cushions in relaxing colours.

2. Now examine your drapes (curtains) or shades (blinds). Are they long enough and wide enough? When closed, do they leave gaps where light can filter through? To encourage maximum sleep time, choose dark-coloured drapes or shades and ensure that the drapes are fully-lined to keep out any light.

3. How comfortable is your bed? Make sure that you have a mattress that suits you, and remember to turn it regularly. Invest in good pillows and cosy bedding so that getting into bed is a delight.

4. Re-organize your cupboards and storage space so that there is no visible clutter. Ban work, your computer, the TV, and anything else that could disturb your mind, but allow yourself to listen to soft music or read a relaxing book, before you try to sleep.

5. Try to create an atmosphere of peace in your bedroom by introducing a special object, such as a calming picture or a beautiful vase. Or burn essential oils, such as lavender, sweet marjoram or ylang ylang, in an aromatherapy burner to promote sleep.

BUILD A NURTURING LIFE

Did you know that the balance (or lack of it) between work and other aspects of your life can have a huge impact on your health? For the past 25 years, Dr Dean Ornish has directed clinical research exploring the impact of various lifestyles on patients with coronary heart disease in the US. He has found that a lifestyle that comprehensively nurtures well-being can begin to reverse even serious coronary heart disease, without drugs or surgery. This discovery holds vital implications for the building and maintenance of well-being in the healthy population at large.

Vast amounts are written about life/work balance. Usually the main message is a simple one: that you have a work life, and you have to balance it out with your home life. Instead, try thinking, "I have a life – a priceless miracle of a life. I must try to make the most of it."

We all have an inbuilt need for mental stimulation; love and intimacy; exercise and good nutrition; connection with our community; spiritual succour; and inspiration. When these needs are met, we feel happy, energetic and healthy. But when one or more is neglected, that aspect of ourselves becomes starved and our happiness and well-being are compromised.

The Faulkner Life Balance Map (opposite) shows you the kinds of things which nurture

THE FAULKNER LIFE BALANCE MAP
practice + integration = transformation

This diagram shows the six "containers of life" which you need to fill, in order to create a richly harmonized way of living. The more you practise regular, long-term activities which fill these life containers, and the more you integrate your containers with one another (see p.74), the more you can achieve success in all areas of your life.

MENTAL
Both right- and left-brain activity

Logical, rational thinking; breadth of vision; problem-solving; dealing with detail through to the bigger picture; decisiveness; clarity of thinking; prioritization; creativity; intuition

PHYSICAL
The care and use of your body

Cardiovascular exercise such as running or swimming; flexibility; building up energy and stamina; nutrition; relaxation; touch therapies, such as massage and shiatsu

EMOTIONAL

Being open to your own emotional life – to love, sensitivity, trust, anger, fear, shame, vulnerability, fun; connecting with others through love and affection

SOCIAL

Sense of belonging to a circle, group or a community; contributing to your community; involvement with culture, politics, voluntary and charity work

SPIRITUAL
Your personal values and beliefs

Your ethical sense; the way in which you find purpose and meaning in life; religious or spiritual practice; meditation; living with integrity and love

SYMBOLIC
Important inspirations in your life

Images; symbols; legends; myths; stories; fables; parables; icons; role models; mentors; gurus; fantasies and dreams that inspire you

these six aspects of our lives. John Faulkner suggests you imagine your life compartmentalized into six containers labelled: mental, physical, emotional, social, spiritual and symbolic. All of these containers can and should interlink.

Here's an example of how one activity can contribute to several of your life containers simultaneously. I love going on sailing trips with my family and friends in warm places around the world. This activity helps fill my Physical container because sailing is a physically demanding sport. It contributes to my Emotional container as I'm with the people I love; it part-fills the Social container because I make up a member of a group and we have a lot of fun together; and it also fills my Symbolic container because for me, personally, the water, wind and sun represent freedom.

Now it's time to take stock of your own life balance. Remind yourself that you participate in many activities, only one of which is the work you do. There are six ways in which you need to nourish and balance your life and you can't expect your work to fulfil all of these. Now is the time to make an assessment of which areas are lacking – see Work Solution 9, opposite.

The first time you do this you will probably find that a couple of your containers are almost full or well-filled, a couple are about half-full and one or two are pretty much empty. The empty ones highlight which aspects of your life are currently undernourished and neglected, perhaps without you even realizing. Once you have found out which areas are lacking, you can take the necessary steps to redress the imbalance and create a more fulfilling life. Try it and see.

WORK SOLUTION 9

Assess Your Life Balance

Assessing your life balance helps you see where your life is rich and fulfilled and where there may be threadbare patches or even holes. This enables you to make decisions about improving the whole fabric of your life. With commitment and discipline, this exercise can help you transform your well-being.

1. Sit somewhere quiet. Taking some paper and a pencil, draw yourself six empty containers, along the lines of those in the Faulkner Life Balance Map (see p.73). Label them in turn Mental, Physical, Emotional, Social, Spiritual and Symbolic, but otherwise leave them blank.

2. Think about your life as it is now, in respect of each of the labels. Which containers (if any) are full to the brim? Which are half full, or even less? Are any of them almost empty? Draw a line across each container, at the level you think correctly represents how full or empty it is at present.

3. Choose the container that is currently the emptiest. Now think carefully: is there any one, specific step you could take which would improve the fullness of that container, and also link in to the other containers, helping to connect and integrate them?

4. Now do some practical and realistic planning regarding how to incorporate the new step into your life. Remember, you need to practise it regularly. Keep a note of your progress in your journal.

5. Later, when your emptiest container is filling well, repeat this exercise and attend to the next emptiest. Don't stop until all your containers are full.

SURROUND YOURSELF
WITH CALM

Your working area may be the place you spend more time than anywhere else in your life – quite a sobering thought! No matter whether you have a huge office with skyline views or a little cubicle to call your own, it's where you work, and there's no doubt that the quality of your workspace can support your sense of calm and well-being and make you more productive, or it can have an adverse affect. You may find it very useful to take the time to evaluate your own working environment; sometimes even one or two small changes can really improve your quality of life at work.

If you're aware that your working environment agitates you in some way, start by assessing your response to your physical surroundings. Sometimes one person's meat is another person's poison – for example, some people enjoy open-plan offices and find them stimulating and companionable, whereas others hate the noise and exposure, and have to build "walls" of potplants to create privacy. Some people like small, self-contained working areas; they enjoy their own little pocket of territory, whereas others find them claustrophobic.

Looking at how your own working space actually functions for you can help in small but important ways. If filing is an intrinsic part of your job, don't keep your filing cabinets hidden away in an inaccessible dark corner. The position of the telephone, the lighting, the height of your desk, the quality of your chair – these are significant details.

WORK SOLUTION 10

Make Your Working Space Work For You

Taking the time to re-evaluate your own working space can pay surprising dividends. Creating a space that works well for you, and also calms you, is a fundamental way of supporting your well-being at work.

1. Sit quietly and think through what actual functions your working space should support: time at a computer, on the telephone, with paper and pencil, filing, sitting talking with people? Write down the main functions.

2. Analyze exactly how well those functions are supported – height of desk, chairs, positioning of equipment, lighting, ventilation. Unless furniture is screwed to the floor, alter anything necessary. Create the quality of environment which will support you.

3. How orderly are you? Put into practice the old adage: "A place for everything, and everything in its place." With a good filing system, you need never have homeless paper lying around. If you don't know about good filing (and it is an art), find an expert filer to advise you.

4. Now add some beauty to your working space. Flowers can transform a utilitarian office – their beauty and aroma provide small moments of delight during a working day. Think what else would give you pleasure and calm your spirit – perhaps photographs of people you love or a beautiful picture?

5. Resolve to maintain your working space with care. It will take only minutes and it will promote a sense of calm and order that will help you realize your potential.

Take the case of the tall manager who suffered chronic lower back pain for years. He put it down to general stress of work, as his back usually improved on holiday. When, following an assessment of his working space, he raised the height of his desk on small wooden blocks, and acquired a better chair, as though by magic, his back pain eased. Your aim should be to create an environment which is ergonomically right for you, so your body can physically move and work without strain.

Hard words have to be said about piles of paperwork. I speak as someone whose desk used to be so snowed under with papers and files, that my cleaning lady said one day: "I can't actually dust your desk, so I've just blown at it." Mess in your working area is, to be blunt, disorganization. It also fosters dust and creates a bad impression. If you think that you don't mind the mess, it's probably because you've never experienced the tranquillity of an orderly working space. A cluttered environment does nothing to create calm around you, nor does it support focus or clarity. For more in-depth advice on how to tackle clutter ruthlessly, see pp.128–9.

There's no doubt that a bad working environment can undermine performance and even well-being. A senior project manager recalls how, as a young engineer, he used to work in an office immediately above a fast-food restaurant. Every breath he took was permeated with the smell of deep-frying. Understandably, his pleasure in the job was undermined by the unpleasant surroundings.

There are, of course, legal requirements concerning the health and safety of employees, and if you believe these requirements are not being met, you must take action. Something like poor ventilation can badly affect the way you feel and work. Don't just complain to colleagues: establish the facts, and speak to someone who can instigate change. The bottom line is that your workplace must meet the minimum legal requirements.

However, perhaps your physical surroundings are fine, but you don't like the atmosphere in which you're working. In this case the problem is to do with relationships, rather than furniture or layout. A relationship that agitates you in some way needs action, even if you're apprehensive at the thought. You'll find many ideas to help you in Chapter 4. Sometimes it's as simple as saying to someone, in private, "I'd be grateful if you'd consider changing the way you (do such-and-such), as it makes me feel (so-and-so)." This takes courage; but often, people have no idea they are being, say, abrasive or undermining.

It is well worth taking time to list the aspects of your workplace that undermine your effectiveness, or enjoyment of your work, then categorize your list into:

• Things you can change or improve. Ask yourself what would improve matters. Think creatively and specifically about positive steps you can take, and make them happen. Even a small change can make a big difference to your comfort and performance.

• Things you can't change. If things are bad, you can try to ignore them, which creates tension; or if things are unbearable you might decide to leave. However, there is another more positive option – if you can't change something yourself, find out who *can* and approach them. Think what *you* would do, and present a list of ideas for them to consider. You never know, they might implement them!

FIND TIME TO CARE
FOR YOURSELF

One thing most working people have in common is that they're always short of time. We live our lives as if we are a hamster on a treadmill, with little time for relaxation and reflection, let alone fun. The week is spent working long hours, coming home exhausted every evening, and trying to fit in time with our partner or family. Then, at the weekend, we have to cram in all the practical things to service the week ahead, such as shopping, laundry, care of the house or apartment, and perhaps one social event. There is literally never a moment to stop.

So, it is hardly surprising that while we look yearningly at the idea of taking time for ourselves, we end up saying "How am I going to manage that? I don't see enough of my family as it is." We could leave it at that; but here are two good reasons why we shouldn't. First, when you work in today's pressurized environment, scheduling time to attend to your well-being is not a luxury, but an absolute necessity. It should be a non-optional part of your timetable, so that you release stress, build energy and safeguard your health on a continuous basis. After all, how can you perform at work to the best of your ability if you are feeling under par? Second, scheduling in time for self-care can always be done. In fact, it is often the people with the most hectic and demanding schedules who successfully build "self-time" into their lives. They are disciplined about time boundaries and guard their self-time slots, especially when they realize the difference it makes to their performance.

WORK SOLUTION 11

Schedule Yourself Into Your Timetable

It takes creativity to make time for self-care in a hectic life, and it can be done. It can feel odd and even self-indulgent to start with; but if you prioritize your well-being in this way for a couple of months, you'll find you have more energy, and you'll feel more grounded and confident.

1. Sit down with your calendar and go through your day-to-day schedule. Look for possible windows of time in which to spend time on yourself, such as at lunchtime; or interfaces, such as end of the working day and early evening. Consider getting up earlier, or putting aside a half-hour slot in the evening. Consider what could work best for you. (If you have a partner or spouse, it's a wise move to talk through the plan with them, too.)

2. Block out a minimum of half-an-hour for yourself somewhere in each day, for the next two weeks.

3. Decide how you want to spend that time and make arrangements accordingly. For example, if you wish to do exercise, take meditation classes, or go for a massage, book up any necessary sessions in advance. If you need to pack any special clothing, make a note in your calendar to get it ready the night before.

4. Be prepared to stick to these self-care times, even if you feel under pressure (usually from yourself) to give them up. Remember, you deserve it. As the days go by, notice which timing works best.

5. At the end of the first week, schedule self-time in your calendar for the next two weeks ahead.

FIND TIME TO CARE FOR YOURSELF

So how then do you set about creating a daily oasis of time to calm your spirit, replenish your energy and improve your performance? Let's be realistic – nobody is going to *give* you time to stop. The only person who can change things is you, yourself, and this is likely to make you think crossly, "But if it were that easy, I'd have done it already." Perhaps the first thing you need to consider is whether you are willing to go through a period of transition, which may feel risky and uncomfortable, while you establish a new set of habits. Because finding time for yourself *can* be done.

Start by asking yourself, "If I gave myself daily 'time out' how would I feel?" Maybe you'd worry at being over-whelmed by work. Well, point out to yourself that work is much better tackled fresh by a rested person, than laboured over by someone who is exhausted and should have gone home hours ago.

Maybe you'd feel selfish. I can't tell you too strongly that when you lead a demanding life, care of yourself has to come first. Otherwise you're short-changing everyone. Remember that wonderful advice "Love thy neighbour as thyself" – notice that it doesn't say "Love thy neighbour while thyself goes down the drain with exhaustion."

Perhaps you'd fear being perceived as a person who gives less than 100 per cent. Of course, there are companies where a macho culture demands ludicrously long working hours. In one such company, there was a manager who had made the brave decision to leave work on time every night, for the sake of himself and his family. Did this result in him being disparaged by his colleagues? Far from it. "It's true that he won't budge on the time when he goes home," said one, "but he gives 110 per cent when he's here."

The bottom line is, how important do you think that it is to take full responsibility for your energy and health? Surely care of yourself has to come first, or you will under-function your way through life. So sort out your priorities.

Make a start by looking at your timetable and seeing where, with good time management, you can book at least thirty minutes to devote solely to your well-being. Every day. (One senior manager I know gets up at 5am to run every morning because he loves the tranquillity and silence.) If you don't wish to get up earlier, you could take a full, relaxing lunchbreak, or set aside an hour during the evening instead. Once you've allocated your daily well-being time, schedule it into your calendar for at least the next month, to give yourself time to establish this new habit firmly in your life.

The next hurdle is to make sure you stick to it. The person most likely to sabotage this time is you, yourself – we all tend to fall back into old habits. So be disciplined about safe-guarding your well-being time. Don't do chores, spend every minute on yourself. If you're unused to caring for yourself, imagine how committed you would be if you were spending this time with a loved one, or an important client. Don't you deserve the same level of attention?

You may think that taking time for yourself will cause major disruptions in your life. This is unlikely – you'll probably find that life doesn't change much. Everything you do now will still get done; the difference is, you'll feel better equipped to do it, and more confident of success.

THINK POSITIVELY, THINK INSPIRATIONALLY

Have you noticed how some people tend to go through life expecting the worst? Invite them for a day at the beach, and they anticipate sunburn, insect bites and sand in the sandwiches, not to mention a traffic jam on the way home. If you think of your friends and colleagues, there are probably some who always give you a lift with their positive attitude to life, and a few whose negative outlook makes your heart sink.

We all have thinking habits, in the same way that we have habits of action – things we always do in the same way, like arriving home from work: greet the family, put the briefcase in a particular place, change our clothes – whatever it is we always do. It's invaluable to get acquainted with your own thinking habits (see pp.40–43). The reason it's so important is that your thinking habits create the entire mental and emotional inner climate that you live in. If you find you always look for the worst, the unfortunate consequence is that you're likely to create a self-fulfilling prophecy.

Mindfully looking for the positive aspects of your life, and developing this as a thinking habit, has a value beyond price. Thinking positively enables you to:

- notice that even hard times contain opportunity
- move forward from difficulties
- counteract negativity in others
- become more open to goodness in others
- cultivate gratitude – there is always something to be grateful for
- feel happy most of the time and enjoy your life

Are there any benefits to thinking negatively? Ask a negative thinker, and first they'll vehemently deny that they think in a negative way – they'll call it "realistic". Then they'll point out how wise it is to be prepared for the worst, so that it can't catch you by surprise. Frankly, this is nonsense. Thinking through the possible downsides of situations can be done briefly as part of positive thinking, then put to one side. Furthermore, a person who insists on thinking negatively actually creates unhealthy physiological consequences in their body. Negative thinking will elicit a flow of stress hormones in the body, whereas positive thoughts stimulate the secretion of feel-good hormones, which in turn support good immune function.

If you've watched the movie of your mind a few times, (see p.43) and you suspect you're inclined to anxious or negative thinking, bring in your Inner Coach to help you (see pp.52–3). The goal is to cultivate a positive attitude. Listen to the kinds of things you habitually say. Banish anything that predicts a bad future, like "I'm dreading today – I just know things aren't going to go well"; instead, try saying "Today will be a challenge – I'm sure we can find ways of moving forward." Avoid gossip, cynicism or destructive criticism, and don't hang out with anyone who has these habits. Pass on positive feedback or compliments. Encourage yourself into thinking positively, until it becomes habitual.

Of course, no matter how positive we manage to be in life there are always occasional times when everything feels a bit flat. Nothing is actually wrong, there's just a lack of inspiration in our lives and nothing exciting appearing on the horizon.

If this ever applies to you, consider taking the time to build your own positive, personal vision or dream for your life. Just as companies have visions of where they're heading, so too do forward-thinking individuals. Having your own personal vision can lift and energize your life, and clarify what's important to you. It can also help you make decisions when you have important choices to make.

The whole point about a personal vision or dream is that it should inspire you – it should feel thrilling and compelling. Thinking about it will give you a sense of deep satisfaction and excitement, and you'll feel a burst of exhilaration in your body. So if, say, you're in a business where you can see that in five years' time, you could be on the board and playing golf regularly with the big guys, but there's no exhilaration at the thought, you've got the wrong vision.

Dreams need to have a time scale attached to them. Are you thinking about a year's time, or three years, or five, or ten? It needs to be far enough ahead to feel like a guiding star, but not so distant as to seem unattainable. You may wonder how realistic you need to make it. Well, who's to say what is "realistic"? Maybe a better guide is whether you have a sense that it could be achievable, even if you can't yet see all the steps to get there. If the answer's yes, and it excites you – there's your vision. You will know when you've hit the jackpot because it will feel "right". You need to spend some time getting acquainted with this feeling by visualizing yourself in your mind's eye realizing your dream. Imagine how you will feel and look; and what you will be doing and saying. Make the picture come alive in your imagination, so you know how it makes you feel.

Once your personal vision has come alive, you then have to consider how to move toward it. Some people take one step at a time from where they start out. Others need to have realized their dream (in their imagination) and look back at how they got there. You might not find an exact route mapped out, but there are likely to be a few clear steps. This is the time to make a plan. Once you've created the vision and filled in what steps you can, it's extraordinary how ideas keep coming. Sometimes unexpected things develop, and your dream broadens, or changes direction; but it will always validate your positive approach to life, inspiring you to fulfil your true potential.

MOVE YOUR LIFE FORWARD

At least one reason why you're reading this book is because you're interested in making fundamental, long-term changes in your life – learning ways of releasing stress from your body and mind, freeing you to become more happy and successful. Moving your life forward in this way is potentially transformational; it's also completely realistic, if you use my tried-and-tested techniques.

Some people like to build long-term change a step at a time. For example, you could expand your exercise portfolio (see pp.60–61), next begin doing meditation (see p.57), then start regular touch therapy (see pp.62–65). This way, you gradually build and consolidate your new approach. Others prefer to take their time absorbing ideas, then make a master plan – and implement it from the word go. Which approach do you feel would suit you?

Creating long-term change needs focus and commitment. You know the way it often is with something new – you're interested, you try out new ideas; but the next time

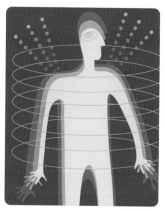

you're under pressure, you switch back into default mode, ending up exhausted and depleted. Make a pledge not to do that this time. If you fall by the wayside occasionally, cut yourself some slack. But do ask yourself how it happened. Was it bad scheduling, or did you allow something else to take precedence? If so, why? What seemed more important? Work out how you could can avoid this in future. Make this the big turning point where you take authoritative charge of your own life.

WORK SOLUTION 12

Building Your Well-being

Now's the time to make a realistic plan to transform your life in general. Take time over this exercise – good planning will create the seedbed for success.

1. Sit quietly and write down the reasons why you want to move your life forward.

2. In the light of what you have learned in this book so far, list all the elements you feel you need in order to release stress and build well-being in your life. You should consider including:

- *deep relaxation or meditation*
- *exercise*
- *touch therapy such as massage*
- *eating healthier food*
- *balancing your work, home and social lives*

3. Decide whether to incorporate these elements a step at a time, or to make a master plan including everything from the beginning.

4. Make a realistic timetable. Book classes or sessions and make all preparations.

5. Commit yourself mindfully. Remember, this is not a trivial undertaking. Make it happen! Maintain your focus and motivation and create a new set of practices that become habitual.

6. Keep a brief journal to review your progress. Start by listing your reasons for wanting to move forward. if you review it after a month, you should be able to see how you have already progressed.

chapter 4

SOUNDS FAMILIAR

At work, people exhibit their own strengths and gifts; they also have their weaknesses and blind spots. There's a certain amount of personal information that they're willing to be open about, but there are other, work-related anxieties that they would rather not disclose. They'd rather appear highly capable at all times. However, many people would be astonished to realize just how many colleagues have similar feelings – we all tend to conceal our worries as best we can.

In this chapter we look at ways to deal with some of the most common problems people have in the workplace. We explore each topic in detail, examining how the situation might have arisen, how it might make you feel, and how it can be addressed. You learn some realistic, workable options for tackling the problems, supported by recommended forms of exercise or relaxation presented in symbols in the margin (only the symbols depicted in full-strength colour apply to that particular problem). A detailed key to the symbols can be found on p.11.

I CAN'T MAKE DECISIONS

Indecision often leads to a kind of mental paralysis, where clarity of thought disappears into an increasingly thick fog. The good news is that through acknowledging your fear of making decisions and then by creating a purposeful strategy for working through that fear, the fog will soon lift.

Start by asking yourself why you find it so hard to make decisions. The cause is nearly always fear that the consequences of the decision will be bad for business or your status. This anxiety usually stems from a self-taught message: "I have to get things right or I will be disparaged." It's time to believe in a new message: the only person who never makes a wrong decision is a person who never makes any decisions.

Good decision-makers are not passive – they acknowledge and learn from even their misguided decisions and then they move on.

Once you have started to overwrite your negative mental messages, you need to take time to develop a strong, rational decision-making process. If you follow a set of self-imposed guidelines on decision-making, you will know that all your decisions were reached in the spirit of considered thought. With practice, the process will become automatic, and decisions will come more quickly and naturally (of course, some decisions always take time – especially if you need to gather information).

Begin your decision-making process by defining the exact decision to be made. Write it down as a question at the top of a piece of paper. Say, "How many units do we need to output this year to meet the target?" Look at it carefully – what information do you need to be able to come to a conclusion? Gather together this information. What are the objectives of your decision? What do you need to gain from it, and what benefits will others expect to gain? For example, your objective might be to meet your annual target, but your team manager's objective might be to ensure that the staff are not overstretched; while your CEO's objective might be to beat the target by 10,000 units. It's worth remembering that you will not be able to meet everyone's objectives all the time, but you will be able to make and support a decision that maximizes compatibility. Classify the objectives into "musts" and "wants". The "musts" have in-built criteria that need to be met, such as a lowest unit price of $5,000; or a minimum output of 100,000 units. The "wants" are not essential, but desirable – list these in order of importance.

Now look into the range of possibilities – perhaps you can just meet the target without overstretching staff, but you could make the extra 10,000 units if you were to employ one more junior (how much would this cost and would it be worth it?). Test whether the various options meet the criteria for the "musts", and discard any that do not. Then test the various decision options against your list of "wants". Complete your analysis by assessing which options best satisfy both the "musts" and the "wants".

Which of your test decisions appears to bring the best results? You are the expert – which would you recommend as the best option? Congratulations – this is your decision!

I CAN'T BE ASSERTIVE

There are people who have no problem at all with being assertive, and there are people who really struggle with it. Neither group has the faintest idea how it feels to be the other way. People who can't assert themselves are usually people who also find it hard to discipline others, to return faulty goods to stores, to recognize when they're becoming over-loaded or to require someone to re-do shoddy work. Take the example of the highly intelligent and talented young man who was practising assertive behaviour in a role play. At first, he just couldn't do it. Instead of sounding natural and author-itative, his voice came out strangled and beseeching. Another member of the group, who had no problem with assertion, said in amazement "I just don't get it. Why can't he just say it?"

In fact, those of us who struggle with assertion have learned, early in our lives, to be over-mindful of others'

feelings. Inside us there is a voice saying "Be nice, it's not OK to upset others." Somehow, we confuse assertion with aggression – although they're utterly different from each other.

A person being assertive is stating clearly a wish, a truth or an opinion: he or she is speaking out with clarity, expressing something they want to be heard, and the purpose is constructive communication. Look how fundamentally aggression differs: an aggressive person is attacking or bullying, with the sole purpose of domination – it's all to do with gaining power. It's right to back off from speaking aggressively. However, assertiveness is to do with speaking your truth, which any human being has the right to do. In the workplace, there are times when having the courage to speak out assertively is not just appropriate, it is necessary. How else can you express clear opinions, demand high standards, correct misconceptions and stand up for what's right?

If you know you struggle to make your voice heard, take heart. You can change this. You could start by simply observing how other people at work "do assertive". They stand or sit quite straight, they make eye contact, they open their mouths and out come the words. Even if they speak with passion, it will be clear, clean, direct, and you'll hear exactly what they think. There is nothing overbearing or bullying in their manner – they are just very direct and truthful.

Then, observe those who can't be assertive. They often try to bottle up what they want to say. But the more they try to hold back, the more they turn themselves into a simmering human volcano – you know the kind of thing, a colleague says to you: "What's the matter with Jenny today? You could cut the atmosphere in her office with a knife." Sooner or later, such people hit the roof, often about something quite small. This isn't assertive behaviour, it's explosive behaviour. It doesn't improve communication, it merely promotes bad feeling; and sadly, it all arises from trying to avoid the healthy, honest practice of being assertive.

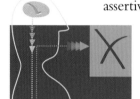

Let's look at what happens when you don't find speaking assertively easy. You feel the words rising in you "This piece of work isn't good enough," or "I can't stay late tonight, it's my anniversary," but what actually comes out is: "This does need more work, but don't worry, I can finish it off" or "Well ... I suppose I could stay for another hour." By backing off you have lost your truthful voice. You then feel completely exasperated with yourself.

Now visualize, in your mind's eye, what happens in the same situations if, magically, you are assertive and reply with the words you want to say. Quite likely you would anticipate being disliked. Do a reality check here: think of times when you have witnessed a colleague asking someone to redo their work or saying "no" in a matter-of-fact way. Did everyone start hating that colleague? Probably not. If anything, people gain respect for someone who can be straightforward.

Now do the exercise opposite. The first time you try this, it may feel like dangerous territory, but don't give up. Handle the feeling and reclaim your voice. The more you practise this, the easier it will become. Speaking your own truth will make you feel stronger and more open to new challenges.

WORK SOLUTION 13

How To Assert Yourself: Move, Breathe, Speak

In the moment you back off from asserting yourself, it's likely you limit your breathing, lose eye contact and hold yourself still inside. Familiarize yourself with this exercise so that the next time you find yourself in a situation where you need to be assertive, you can follow these steps – they work.

1. Move your body: if you're sitting down, shift in your chair; if you're standing up, change your stance. This will unfreeze you. As you move, take your eyes away from the person you're talking to, take a deep breath, then release it. (This will take about 2 seconds. It won't seem odd, just as though you're reflecting momentarily.)

2. Now take another deep breath, make direct eye contact and speak. If you need more time to ground yourself, start with a phrase to buy you time, such as: "I'm not happy about this," or "We're going to have to find another way."

3. The other person will realize you've got something important to say. Keep breathing and, with conscious courage, say what you need to say – directly and simply. Then stop and wait.

4. Don't be apologetic or meek, and don't justify yourself. Say nothing else.

5. If you are challenged and you have to stand your ground, just repeat what you said before. Don't back down, just keep breathing slowly and evenly.

6. The first few times you do this, notice that being assertive doesn't lead to doom and destruction, rather it frees your energy and makes you feel stronger. Each time you manage to be assertive in this way, celebrate your success (privately).

I CAN'T COMMUNICATE EFFECTIVELY

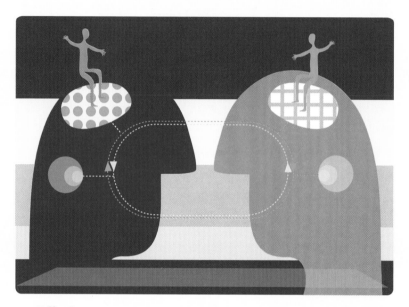

Effective communication is a two-way business. Have you ever been speaking to a colleague, and suddenly noticed that they're not actually listening, they're only waiting to put across their own opinion? Think of using a radio-telephone where you have to be on either "transmit" or "receive". A good conversation, even a brief one, contains *both* "transmit"*and*"receive". In a low-calibre exchange of the kind that happens in offices every day, that doesn't happen. Maybe you have a mountain of work to get through and an equally rushed colleague is trying to convince you of something you don't agree with. In fact, all you want to do is make him or her realize that they are wrong so you can get on.

What happens is that you both go on "transmit". There's a lot of interrupting, your attention is on your own view, you get critical and try to rush the other person into dropping their point; and in the meantime, they're doing the same to you. Even worse, maybe they're not naturally assertive, so you succeed in forcing through your opinion. You got your way, and you can get on. Success? No.

Let's look at some of the possible results of this kind of exchange. You may make wrong assumptions about the other person's motives. You are likely to misinterpret what they say if you haven't listened fully, so you may form an opinion based only on partial information. You might then criticize their point of view – and that will annoy them and reduce their respect for you. All in all, there's no sense of rewarding collaboration. Both sides feel frustrated, annoyed and physically tense because their communication failed.

By contrast, really effective listening is such a rare skill that when it *is* employed, it usually improves profoundly the quality of relationships between the listener and his or her colleagues, engendering respect, trust and loyalty. Listening well employs a set of skills that you can practise and develop. It begins with accepting that for the next few minutes, you're going to *take time* to do something *valuable*. If time is limited, say "I only have ten minutes, but I'd like to find out more from you ... ." Put your own view on hold for now. The main priority is to gain insight.

Listen without interruption. Breathe slowly and keep eye contact. Be curious. If you don't understand something, *ask*; if you're mystified by your colleague's disagreement about something, *ask*. If you notice yourself starting to feel argumentative, *ask more*. Repeat back to them the main thrust of

what they've said. This ensures you've understood correctly, and it also relaxes them because they know they've been heard. You are likely to feel calm and energized too. You have new food for thought, and even if you don't agree with your colleague, at least you are better informed.

However, what if your problem is not listening, but the way you communicate information to others? This could well be the case if other people often have a problem understanding what you're getting at, or if they often seem to misunderstand or get impatient. Start to tackle the problem by asking a trusted colleague for feedback about how you get it wrong. Listen to what they have to say without becoming defensive. Note down their comments and suggestions.

Expressing ourselves well is almost impossible if we aren't clear why a particular communication is necessary and what we hope to gain from it. Always keep in mind your objectives and expectations – and always articulate them. This way you are less likely to become rambling or muddled, and more likely to get the results you need.

If you have time to prepare, make notes on the essentials that you want to get across and why. Summarize the key points, supported if necessary by facts, figures and opinion. Ask your listener if anything needs clarifying (if you are giving a brief, ask them to repeat back what they have to do for you). If you find it easier to express yourself on paper, offer a copy of your notes to the listener, just to be on the safe side.

WORK SOLUTION 14

Learn To Be "On Receive"

Listening effectively takes practice. However it is worth persevering until you master this worthwhile skill because it can transform relationships, improve interactions and boost productivity levels in your workplace.

1. Look out for a chance to become better informed and improve your relationship with someone at work by listening effectively. For example, a good opportunity might be when you notice that you're feeling rather agitated or being particularly stubborn during a conversation with a colleague.

2. Put your own view totally to one side – what you are doing now is gathering information. Decide that you will invest a certain amount of time in this.

3. Don't do anything else at the same time. Listen with all your attention – show this in your body language by making eye contact and facing the speaker. By listening with such focus, you are transmitting the powerful and positive message: "I am interested, I want to understand your position."

4. Don't interrupt or comment or finish your colleague's sentences. If something isn't clear, ask them to explain in more detail until you really understand what they are trying to say.

5. Summarize their points and repeat them back to the person. If you have understood correctly, you'll see them nodding and relaxing.

6. If you need time to reflect, say so, and thank them for their input. Then, ask yourself: what have I learned? How do I feel? How have things changed?

I CAN'T ACCEPT CRITICISM

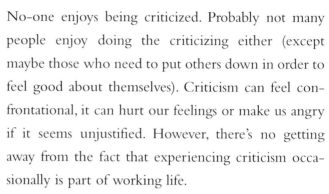

No-one enjoys being criticized. Probably not many people enjoy doing the criticizing either (except maybe those who need to put others down in order to feel good about themselves). Criticism can feel confrontational, it can hurt our feelings or make us angry if it seems unjustified. However, there's no getting away from the fact that experiencing criticism occasionally is part of working life.

A criticism is someone's opinion about us – our actions or behaviour. They are disagreeing with the way in which we've acted or behaved, and telling us so. Depending on how the criticism is delivered, this can feel like a valid and constructive point or an unjustified attack. If it's the latter, our initial reaction is often defensive. We tend either to retreat and feel demolished and mortified, or else to come out fighting, trying to defend our position.

Always remember that criticism is just someone's opinion, and however clumsily it may have been delivered, there may be information in it that you should hear. It's not, or shouldn't be, an attack on your value as a human being. So if you can, take an emotional step back, and listen with interest. What are they saying? How does it differ from your own perception? Has their criticism cast light on something that has been a blind spot for you? Can you understand why they said it? How do they think things should be different?

In other words, try not to channel your energy into feeling attacked. Instead, treat the situation as a learning opportunity, with a potentially positive outcome.

WORK SOLUTION 15

What Can I Learn Here?

The next time you are criticized at work, try to distance yourself from the criticism so that you aren't hurt or angered unduly by it, but you can still explore whether there is something to be learned from it.

1. When you hear the criticism, you'll probably respond both physically and emotionally. You may find that your breath becomes shallow and your body releases epinephrine (adrenalin) as you experience, in effect, a shock. You may feel defensive, upset or angry. Observe these responses in yourself without attaching yourself to them; then, consciously deepen your breathing in order to calm yourself.

2. A personal attack on you as a human being is never defensible; but constructive criticism of the way you handled something is different, and could be helpful. Listen with care. Establish exactly what the criticism is – what did you (in their opinion) get wrong? What (in their opinion) might have been better? Or how would they like you to do things differently in future?

3. Take some time for reflection. Thank the person for their comments and ask for clarification if anything is unclear. Tell the person that you'd like to think about what they've said and get back to them with some solutions. Schedule a time for them.

4. Reflect upon what was said. Remember that this criticism may have thrown you into the Change Journey (see pp.46–7). Has this given you any insights? Decide what specific learning you would like to carry forward from the encounter. If you feel strongly that a certain point is unjustified, think how you might state your case while accepting the point that was made. Perhaps this is your opportunity to see things in a new perspective and find a conclusion acceptable to all concerned?

I CAN'T EXPRESS FEELINGS AT WORK

Are you someone who believes strongly that people should take only their rational, task-focused selves to work, and keep feelings for home? Would you cringe at the idea of saying or doing anything heartfelt in your workplace? Does the sight of a colleague obviously in distress make you want to disappear through the nearest door? If so, you're not alone.

Now, take a moment to explore the limitations you are placing on your potential. However rational you are, you also have feelings at work – we all do. What about the exhilaration of success, or the disappointment of failure? What about boredom, or excitement, or outrage if something feels unfair or unethical? Your feelings, and everyone else's, are part of the work picture. Ignoring that fact can lead to stress and reduced effectiveness.

Great leaders don't lead simply with their rational intellects, they lead also with their emotions, their souls, their passion and their intuition. Consider some of the roles that need to be approached with heart. What about when you really need your staff to stretch targets – to perform outstandingly? People only do this if they're inspired; and inspiration comes when we feel not only challenged but believed-in, respected and encouraged – messages from the heart, not the intellect. Similarly, how do you support your team when they've had a disappointing setback? They probably already know *why* things have gone wrong. What they need now is sympathy, encouragement and help to set things in perspective so that they can move forward. This is where your heart plays its part – logic on its own isn't enough.

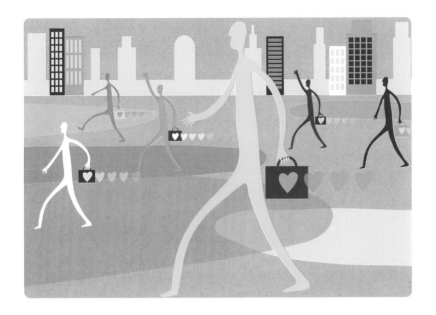

So, how do you start to allow your heart to play its part at work? The answer is to practise small ways of improving contact with your colleagues, one step at a time. For example, you can begin by saying a warm good morning to everyone and by remembering to thank people who do work for you. You can transform the way you listen (see pp.98–101), but perhaps one of the most effective ways is to go on walkabouts – informal information-gathering exercises, to learn small non-work facts about your team. You can then follow up with, for example: "How did your wife's operation go?" or, "How was the tennis tournament at the weekend?" You must also be prepared to disclose a little about yourself in exchange. You may be amazed at the change that occurs when you start to relate to people as complex human beings with feelings. As one manager put it: "We seem to be pulling together much better as a team now; and I'm beginning to understand who it is that I'm leading."

I CAN'T MANAGE
TIME EFFECTIVELY

"If only every day had an extra two or three hours", said a tired project manager, "my problems would be solved. I always have too much to do." He was already working in the

evenings and at weekends. Actually, he could have filled any available extra time with work because his problem was bad time-management. He confused being busy with being effective, which meant that he often dealt with the most urgent task, rather than the most important.

If you suspect that better time management could transform your working life, start by observing and logging what you do now, for two weeks. Ask yourself the following questions: do you tend to respond to the most immediate task, rather than plan ahead in detail? When you do plan ahead, do the tasks take longer or shorter than you expected? How often are you diverted by interruptions? How much time do you spend on routine tasks – could you delegate them? During which part of the day do you work best? What seem to be your problem areas? Record your answers to these questions daily. After you have done this for two weeks, the weak areas in your current time management should be evident – you might be surprised by the results. As that tired project manager commented "I had no idea of how many interruptions I just allowed to happen, such as 'phone calls, impromptu meetings or attending personally to problems I could have delegated. Never again."

If this type of thing rings true for you, don't worry. You can easily improve the situation, if you're prepared to bring into your worklife some planning, clarity and singlemindedness. The guidelines below are tried-and-tested; stick to them as closely as possible for a full month, and you'll never want to go back to haphazard time management again. To become your own time management expert:

• Map out your schedule the day before, or even the week before. Use the first few minutes of each morning to note your tasks and priorities for that day; take care to prioritize the most important, not the most urgent tasks.

• Tackle the hardest things first, not last. Just take a deep breath and take the plunge. You will feel good because you're getting to grips with the problems.

• Make your objectives clear, challenging and realistic. When planning a new task or project break it down into achievable steps; establish how you will measure progress; clarify service level agreements with other departments; consult with colleagues and your boss, and agree appropriate time-scales to achieve interim goals; plan for things to go wrong – the best-laid plans can be de-railed for unforeseeable reasons.

• Say no when you need to – be direct, courteous and firm (see pp.94–7 for advice on how to be assertive).

• Avoid, limit or control interruptions, time-stealers and red herrings.

• Delegate with authority and trust (see pp.124–7).

CONSTANT INTERRUPTIONS
DRIVE ME MAD

You know the kind of day – looking ahead, it seems straightforward enough: emails and correspondence to attend to, a report to draft, a proposal to complete, several meetings. However things don't go as planned. There's one interruption after another. You've no sooner begun a task than someone's at the door or on the 'phone, various things have cropped up and you seem to spend most of your day trying to retrieve your focus. Nothing gets finished.

Studies have shown that constant interruptions are the single most annoying element of a manager's day. As one frustrated marketing manager said, "It sometimes gets to the stage where I want to hang up a notice saying GO AWAY, lock my office door and put in ear plugs. That way, I might finally get some work done."

Why are interruptions so maddening? We can boil it down to two basic reasons. The first is that we've created a mental picture of how we'll spend our time, with clear expectations of things we'll complete or deal with; in other words, we've defined what will represent success. When we are constantly interrupted, our day or our week pans out differently, and the mismatch between our expectation and reality makes us feel that we've failed. The second reason is that interruptions thwart a very human pleasure – satisfaction in completing a job well done, however small.

If there are times when you seriously need to have no interruptions, you have to take action. Negotiate with colleagues that during those times, you'll use a signal: for example, you'll close your door, you'll wear headphones, or as in the case of one young IT project manager who was driven mad by interruptions during complex programming procedures, put a little red flag on top of your computer, which indicates "Please come back later." A good compromise is to try to complete at least one or two tasks before making yourself available to others. This will give you some satisfaction and also help you feel more relaxed.

In fact, if you are the manager of a team, ask yourself whether those queries and requests really are interruptions. Could they be, in fact, your team seeking leadership from you? Accepting that dealing with interruptions is part of your role (if it is), and planning accordingly, can remove most of the frustration from the situation. So, try scheduling "interruption time" into your day. There need not be a set time during which people can approach you, just an assumption on your part that, say, two hours of your day will be spent dealing with unplanned and unexpected interactions.

You might also like to consider working flexible hours to help you get through your core work. For example, rather than working late, a civil engineer with a heavy workload goes into work very early a couple of times a week so that he can get most of his own work done before his staff and colleagues arrive. Others find that working from home one day a week is a good solution, but only if their home can offer the necessary peace and privacy.

I'VE GOT TOO MUCH
ON MY PLATE

A senior manager was once telling me how seriously and chronically overloaded he felt, when he shocked himself (and me) by confessing "Do you know, I wouldn't mind being run over or something – not being drastically injured, just, say, breaking a leg quite badly. Then I'd *have* to have a few weeks off."

If you have too much on your plate and it's not a temporary state of affairs, you must take action. Remember, chronic pressure of this kind damages your health. First, think things through. How has this overload happened? For example, are you saying "no" enough? If not, is that because you find it difficult to assert yourself (see pp.94–7)? Is it because you want your seniors to think you have a boundless capacity for work? Or is it because you believe that no-one else can do the work? Actually, the reality is that if you did break a leg, things would either still get done, or else they wouldn't get done – either way, life would move on. The fact is none of us is indispensable.

So take a short time to become really well-acquainted with how you operate when you're seriously overstretched. Note the way your mind works – how you are thinking (see pp.34–43). Also, assess the way your body feels (see pp.30–33). Once you become conscious of the symptoms of work overload, you're more likely to recognize when it starts to happen again, and you'll be in a good position to take action long before the situation gets this bad.

The next step is to discuss the situation with your boss. If you hang back from this because you don't want him to know you're human and overworked, you need to examine this type of thinking. How can we expect others to value and respect us, if we won't value and respect ourselves? So don't be afraid to speak up. Don't be even slightly defensive, simply be factual and provide evidence of how you have far more on your plate than one hard-working person can be expected realistically to deal with. If you feel that this sounds negative, suggest some ideas for positive solutions, agree on priorities and strategies and book another meeting for a month's time in which to review the situation.

When you've been struggling with work overload for a while, it's likely that your life balance is also out of kilter. Having agreed a realistic way forward with your boss, also assess what you need to do to make your life in general more satisfying and relaxing. Work Solution 9 on p.75 will help you with this. If you've been working late every night, stop. Simply don't do it. For the next month, work only in a grounded, sustainable way. Remember to delegate. Bear in mind, too, that to aim for perfection is unnecessary – tell yourself that you will settle for doing a very good job. To begin with, your body chemistry (which will have been on red alert for ages) may send anxious messages to your brain, such as: "This can't be right! Surely I ought to be going flat out?" So include regular, supportive exercise in your timetable as you rebalance your life.

I CAN'T JUGGLE WORK
AND HOME

Balancing the demands of work with the needs of home, especially if you have a family, can be a minefield. It seems that guilt goes with the territory, whichever way you cut it. This is true for both men and women. It's poignant to hear business people, who work punishing hours and maybe travel as part of their job as well, speak of their dilemmas. They often feel guilty at being home so late or so little; and yet the long hours and absences are all part of the job, which allows them to support their family.

Even without travelling, the sheer demands of a working day mean that when you arrive home, you're ready to wind down and relax – but if you have children, you salvage what's left of your energy to try to be a good parent and spend some quality time with them. Most people do the best they can out of love; but it's a demanding way to live. And if it's tough on men, it can be even tougher on women – studies of full-time working couples show that frequently it's still the women who take on a greater share of the domestic work and child care.

Why is it that we allow our work to have such an impact on our home life? Perhaps, because many of us have been brought up to strive and do our best, with no advice on how to maintain sanity and balance in our lives; or perhaps we are simply slow to notice what is happening. Either way, the emotional pressure of feeling you have too many balls in the air can feel relentless. What's more, it will carry on that way unless you do something about it.

Overhauling your life needs some serious thinking through. To help you make an action plan, write a list of all the work pressures that impact on your home life. For example, does working at weekends mean that your partner has to do most of the domestic chores? Is working late putting your relationship under strain? Now rank them according to how much angst they are causing you. Starting with the one that worries you most, try to find a creative solution for each stressor. For example, if you really need to attend occasional meetings at your child's school, can you negotiate to work flexible hours on the days when the meetings are held?

When you have finished, run your eye down the list and see whether a pattern emerges. Could you manage your time better (see pp.106–7)? Could several of your problems be solved by the same solution, such as working "flexi-time" every day? Should you be saying "no" to your boss more often when he or she tries to give you more work (see pp.94–7)? Could you delegate more (see pp.124–7)? Would it relieve pressure if you created more organization in your life (see pp.76–9 and pp.128–9) by establishing good systems for everything, from your filing through to your laundry?

Making two or three small but significant changes can make all the difference between a completely pressurized, work-oriented life and a better balanced one, where your home life is given the respect and importance it deserves. As any good boss recognizes, your workplace will get better value from you if you're happier, healthier and less stressed.

MY BOSS GIVES ME NO AUTONOMY

The degree of autonomy that people are comfortable with varies from one person to another. Some people are reassured by strict targets and lots of monitoring because they are inexperienced or because their confidence in their own judgment is not high. On the other hand, experienced team members who are competent and sure of their ground don't need "tight" management: after the initial briefing, they want and expect to be able to make their own judgments and decisions.

If this sounds like you, you will know that if your boss doesn't give you that autonomy, it can become deeply demotivating – you feel that your boss doesn't trust or respect your judgment and your energy and enthusiasm for the job drain away.

This situation must be addressed. The relationship you have with your boss is of fundamental importance to your ability to perform well within your role, and to develop yourself professionally; it's probably your most important working relationship.

A boss who holds the reins too tightly for your liking might do this for several reasons. Perhaps he or she simply doesn't realize that you'd like more autonomy – they may have developed a "tight" management style because in the past their staff have flourished that way. Or, they may be anxious that you won't do the job properly (this is not necessarily an indictment of your abilities, it may just indicate that they have been let down before). Or then again, they may be anxious that if things don't go well, it will reflect badly on them; so they only feel safe running the show on an over-tight rein.

Before you speak to your boss, think about your relationship as it stands. Which parts work well? Is there a way you can build on these? If you sense that your boss's reluctance to give you autonomy stems from anxiety about results, consider what would help to relieve it. For example, are you clear what the boss's key objectives are? What support can you give toward achieving these? What are his or her priorities? If they place a high value on, say, customer care, be prepared to make this your priority too, and make sure that you do nothing that seems to conflict with it.

Next, speak to your boss. Explain that you feel de-motivated by lack of autonomy; say you love a challenge, and you would appreciate the opportunity to show what you can do. Propose a schedule of meetings in which to report back – these will keep your boss informed sufficiently to reassure him or her. Make sure that you are both clear about boundaries of responsibility between you – don't leave the meeting until you have mutually agreed and made a record of what decisions you are allowed to make. Categories should include decisions you can make after discussion; on your own, but reporting to the boss afterward; and on your own with no need to report. If you are scrupulous about consulting and reporting back, it's likely that your boss will expand your autonomy over time, as trust is built up between you.

I NEVER GET CONSULTED

A successful account manager returned to work six months after having a baby, ready for a three-day week and looking forward to it. She slipped back into her role with ease; but she found an unexpected and unwelcome change. "Just because I now work part-time," she said, "I'm not consulted about changes. Decisions are made in my absence, which I suppose is understandable; but the worst thing is that nobody actually thinks to inform me about those decisions. I usually find out about them by accident. It's as though I don't count as much as I used to."

Not being consulted can make you feel disregarded, and even disrespected. If you're accustomed to having your voice heard, you may feel frustrated and angry because the message seems to be "Your view has no importance, so we're not concerned about what you think". And if you don't have a highly developed sense of self-esteem, it can seem that your lack of self-belief is simply being confirmed. In circumstances where you are not being consulted, it's important not to let your fantasies take over. This is the time to use your rational self to consider the likely reasons why you're being bypassed.

It may be because you're not there – if, for example, you're part-time, or you're often out of the office with clients, or you sometimes work from home. None of these is a valid reason for you to be bypassed, but it happens. Colleagues can become so focused on what's in front of them that they fail to communicate properly. Other reasons why people aren't consulting you could include that they don't realize you have a contribution to make, particularly if you are new to the department, or if you're a person who generally tends to listen rather than speak out. Sometimes managers even consciously exclude people from the decision-making process simply because they are intent on driving things through *their* way.

When you have worked out why you think you're not being consulted, the next step is to speak out. But don't complain to your peers, who are in no position to help. Go to the person who can change the situation. Avoid sounding angry or injured – you will come over as negative. Point out how you are not being consulted and say something brief about the demotivating effect this is having on you. Then move on to offer some positive ideas, which demonstrate how your contribution could be both relevant and valuable.

If you're often out of the office, suggest a strong, workable way to keep in communication, which everyone would be willing to adhere to. If you've simply been disregarded, state that you'd like to develop a contributing voice, as you feel you've got lots to offer, and give examples. Make yourself sound like an interesting, positive person to include in the decision-making process.

When you've successfully established new protocols or raised your profile in this way, really put your energy into sustaining the positive changes and making them work. Make it worthwhile for your colleagues to consult you – in this way your opinion will become established and valued.

NO-ONE CARES OR
TRIES TO HELP ME

Prolonged pressure needs skilful self-management; it's made much worse if you feel isolated or unsupported. Even the strongest person needs good support structures in place. If you feel as though no-one cares or tries to help you, this needs some action.

The first thing to explore is whether this unsupported feeling is a product of your own unmanaged stress. Try doing Work Solution 4 on p.43 a few times, to help you understand the directions your mind habitually follows. Perhaps anxiety is making you try to do everything yourself? Maybe you're someone who backs off from contact with others when you're under extreme pressure? Many people do this, and it creates a sense of isolation. Better stress management will bring you back in contact again.

If you're sure you should be getting better support, you need to put this across in a clear, factual way. Beware of coming across as a victim, as people will back off from any suggestion of "poor me" – they have their own pressures to deal with. An effective manager will care about your well-being and about the job being done properly, and he or she should be willing to establish support for your role if necessary.

So think things through: should you be having help? Should someone be doing more for you? Is there someone whose role should include showing interest in your concerns and giving you support, but it's not happening? Or is there no-one with that responsibility?

Either way, it's helpful first to get clear in your own mind exactly what your needs are. Treat it as a small but vital project that needs a positive outcome. Make a very specific list of what input you believe would help you, when and how often. Be factual and make sure you don't sound as if you are feeling sorry for yourself. Also include an estimate of how much your effectiveness or productivity would improve if the support were in place.

Next, consider who needs to hear this information, and perhaps more importantly, who is in a position to do something about it. Make an appointment to discuss the situation with them. If the person you're talking to is the person who should be giving the guidance or help, don't fall into the trap of watering down your message because you are loath to appear critical. By the same token, don't sound blaming or complaining. Instead, be straightforward and matter-of-fact – this makes it less personal and easier for them to hear.

Of course, they may simply not have noticed the situation, as was the case with a project manager, who handled her workload with such competence that more and more was passed her way. The volume of work became such that she wisely spoke to her manager, saying that, while she did not wish to give up any of the projects, she would have to extend deadlines if she was to manage them alone. When her manager focused on her actual workload, he was surprised at how much she had to do, and he immediately removed sufficient for things to become manageable again.

I'M STUCK IN A RUT

Realizing that you're stuck in a rut is something that tends to creep up on you. As the weeks roll by, with every day predictable and the work so familiar that you could do it in your sleep, there's nothing exactly wrong. There's even a certain comfort in knowing the territory so well. However, over time, a kind of unease sneaks in. There's no interest or challenge in the day ahead and it gradually dawns on you that you're bored and frustrated.

The only person who can change the situation is you. So once you realize you're stultifying, begin by thinking things through: how did you get in this situation? How can you move forward? Is there a role you could see yourself moving into? Or is there a way you could develop the role you have? When you feel ready, speak to your boss. He or she may not have realized that you're stagnating. Be positive and enthusiastic about developing yourself; and also be very clear that you wish to move out of the rut. Often, this impetus is enough to improve the situation.

However, if you feel you need a major change, then be radical. Compile a portfolio of your skills and experience. Then ask yourself what new challenge would excite you. What would you need to do to make it happen (see Work Solution 16 opposite)? By going in a new direction you are pitching yourself into the Change Journey (see pp.46–7), so include good self-care to help you sustain your energy and drive to achieve a more fulfilling and successful career.

WORK SOLUTION 16

Build Your Vision

When you are stuck in a rut, it can be helpful to take some time to analyze what it is you really want. Building your own vision can give you a renewed sense of purpose and the drive to bring it to a successful realization.

1. Begin by considering what feels really important to you. Make two closely related lists. Call the first your "Needs" – this covers everything from practical needs (such as an income and a home) to personal needs (such as the need to make a difference; for autonomy; to be creative, and so on). The second list is your "Values" – this covers everything that matters to you as a person who tries to live with integrity from an ethical base. Give yourself time to compile these lists, maybe several days. You are "tilling the soil" for your vision.

2. When your lists are complete, establish the deadline by which you hope to have achieved your vision – perhaps one year, or three or five, or even ten years. Then sit quietly, close your eyes and allow yourself some magical thinking: "If I could wave a wand, this is how I would be in X years' time ... ." Don't be over-rational here. Go with the idea that excites you most and imagine yourself living out your vision. Notice how you look, feel, act and so on.

3. Coming back to where you are now, break down the steps you need to take in order to realize your vision. For example, if you see yourself as a director of the company in, say, five years' time, map out the steps or staging posts you need to achieve between now and turning your vision into reality.

4. Take that first step now!

I DON'T KNOW
WHAT'S EXPECTED OF ME

Sometimes we find ourselves in a situation where, through no fault of our own, we are expected to get on with the job, even though we haven't been briefed properly. Take the case of the senior manager who was transferred to a new department, a move he welcomed. The first couple of weeks weren't easy, as his new boss was away when he arrived, but he got on with the job as best he could. The next few weeks were hectic. Time passed; and amazingly, he somehow never got to have an induction meeting of any kind.

After a few months, he complained, "The embarrassing thing is, I don't really know what my boss expects of me. I'm guessing." Of course the most straightforward way was simply to ask; but he felt that this would make him feel foolish after so much time. To protect his feelings we came up with a different strategy. He was to book a meeting with the boss in which to lay out his thinking about forthcoming work, and, at the same time, give himself the opportunity to ask her if this thinking aligned well with her longer-term planning. This meant that if he *was* on the wrong track, his boss could then put him straight.

The message here is obvious: when you're in a new situation, your number one priority should be to insist on becoming fully informed as to what's expected of you. If things change, keep asking questions until you're absolutely clear. No decent manager will object to this – they themselves should, of course, be making sure that you are briefed properly, but sometimes when people are very familiar with

a set-up or a process, they forget how alien it can be to new people. Don't imagine that if you ask a lot of questions in the early days, it makes you look incompetent – quite the opposite. It's an intelligent response to a new situation.

An alternative, when there seems to be no clearcut answer to what's expected of you, is to move yourself out of "anxious child" mode and instead decide for yourself what to do and why. Think everything through and draw up a plan, using all the information available to you. You can't, of course, do this in a vacuum. When you've developed your thinking, take time to discuss it with other interested parties to check that they are broadly in agreement, that they will back you, and whether there's anything you may have overlooked. (Choose carefully whom you trust. Don't approach anyone who might benefit from your failure.)

In a scenario where you know what your job entails, but you're not certain what's expected in terms of workload or targets – again, take the initiative yourself. Of course, you want to get things right and impress your boss. However, if you aren't given clear guidelines about what's expected of you, remind yourself that you're a competent adult. Assess for yourself what level of performance feels fundamentally right. If you ask "How high should I jump?", most bosses can't help answering "Higher", unless they've developed an enlightened approach to the well-being of their staff. So apply common sense and work out for yourself what's realistic and will also make you feel proud.

I CAN'T DELEGATE

Are you a perfectionist – someone who cares passionately about every detail of the project, and delivers a 100-per-cent, immaculate job? If so, you probably have an ongoing struggle. When deadlines loom – exactly when we have the most urgent need to delegate – we often find it hardest to put our faith in others to do a proper job.

This is a disabling mindset that we have to challenge, otherwise we will only exhaust ourselves and demotivate our team. As one hard-working, responsible man whose boss couldn't delegate commented angrily, "She can't trust me to complete work on time. She keeps checking up on me, and it's making me feel like an incompetent ten-year-old." His boss's anxiety was translating into pernickety and interfering behaviour. Capable, committed colleagues can feel irritated and even insulted when it appears that we don't trust them to do a good job.

If you struggle with delegation, recognize that the under-lying problem is that you're anxious about failing. Somewhere along your life's journey, you've absorbed the message that failure is not an option, so you'll do anything to avoid it. No-one wants to fail in life; but the fact is, failures happen to most of us from time to time, and the important thing is to learn from them, then let them go.

Being able to delegate is an absolutely necessary skill in today's workplace. So start with a reality check. Consider whether there's anyone who, in the past, has proved themselves unreliable, and if so, don't delegate to them. Having eliminated those who have already let you down, you need to plan how to delegate to those you *can* trust.

If you know someone who's a good and relaxed delegator, ask them how they do it. Remember that your own anxiety is one of the elements that must be factored into the planning. So until you are more experienced at delegation, build in spacious deadlines, so that if your worst fantasies come true, there's time to salvage the situation. It's always wise to build "hiccup-time" into your planning; but don't underestimate your colleagues – they probably want to meet expectations, not ignore them. You're not the only one interested in doing a good job!

You could also consider coming clean with your team. Tell them you need to rely on them, and that delegation doesn't come easily to you; ask them for an assurance that they will be absolutely dependable in meeting the deadlines. Tell them you need regular, accurate updates on progress and be appreciative when you receive them. Then back off and let them get on with the job.

This will make you anxious, I guarantee. You'll find yourself wondering "What if …", and your body will tense up. You may have an almost irresistible urge to check how things are going, but resist you must. This is the cutting edge of your learning. When things go well or even better, you'll find yourself relaxing deeply as you discover the satisfaction of working with the support of a good team.

I'M THE ONLY PERSON I CAN TRUST

If you have problems delegating (see pp.124–5) one of the reasons why is probably that you find it hard to trust your staff. To be able to trust colleagues you have to believe that they'll be reliable and truthful, that they won't go behind your back, and that they won't let you down. Conversely, if you believe that you can't trust them, you imply that every one of them is unreliable, dishonest or lazy. That could be true, but it is unlikely.

So, if you genuinely find it difficult to trust colleagues, you need to look at why. Do you have a hard job trusting people in general? Do you dislike delegating because you like to remain in control? Or is it a question of "I can't rely on anyone. If I want anything done properly, I have to do it myself"? In this case, you have set high standards for youself, and you find it unacceptable when others don't match up to your expectations. But if you retreat into frustration and anger, you both isolate yourself and alienate your colleagues.

No-one who's part of a team can work in isolation. If, say, you're assembling a report that has input from several people, trusting everyone to make their contribution is all part of the process. Consciously look for reliability in others, and praise it when you find it. Of course, if someone delivers work that's not up to the agreed standard, you are right to feel frustrated. But instead of re-doing it yourself, try pointing out where they have let you down; then, offer constructive criticism and tell them you trust them to redo it adequately.

WORK SOLUTION 17

Trusting Others To Do Their Job

Working with others is an inevitable part of business life. Allowing yourself never to trust others is a recipe for overload and tension. So take steps to loosen the grip of your anxiety and discover the talent and reliability of your colleagues.

1. Take a pen and some paper and draw as many columns as there are people in your team or under your management. Write the name of one person at the top of each column. Now, taking each column in turn, list each person's strengths. Next, go back through the columns and repeat the process, this time writing down each person's weaknesses.

2. Now think about your own job and all that it entails. What tasks are you not able or prepared to entrust to anyone else? Jot them down and put them aside. Next, consider the aspects of your job that you *would* be prepared to delegate, if the person carrying out the task worked under your guidance. Write these down, too. Finally, list any jobs you would be willing to trust others to do, without your input.

3. Analyze and digest the information you have gathered. Think about which qualities are needed to carry out the jobs you are happy to delegate. Then, consult the notes you made on your staff's strengths and weaknesses and try to match each task with the person best suited for the job. For example, Maria, the Sales Administator, might be the best choice for dealing with customer queries because she has strong verbal communication skills, and so on.

4. Start by first entrusting people to do the jobs that don't need your input. Then, gradually delegate more and more. This will lighten your workload, give you more time to sort out any problems and, importantly, make your staff feel more valued.

I CAN'T MANAGE CLUTTER

Do you work surrounded by clutter? Do you hear yourself saying defensive things, such as "I know exactly where everything is – I could find you any document from these piles of paper within seconds"? Sometimes you hit lucky and lay your hands on the document quickly; other times you have

to turn everything upside down to locate a missing file. Once in a while something important disappears for ever. Does this scenario ring a bell?

Some people naturally run a "volcano desk", where everything immediately in front of them is hot and "of the minute". As things are superseded in importance, they get pushed gradually to the edge of the desk where they cool like lava, and eventually end up filed away or in the wastepaper basket. This is not a good working system, as vital documents can get forgotten and lost easily among the cooling lava. It can also become extremely frustrating for others as records of decisions get lost in the files.

Are there any upsides of clutter? For some people, it's just the way they've always been; they don't know how it feels to be orderly. Many people (without realizing it) use a cluttered desk as a barricade – a demonstration of "Look how busy I am – don't give me anything more at present". However, you should think seriously about the impression that you are giving to others. To the non-cluttered population, a cluttered desk is just indisputable evidence of disorganization. There's nothing endearing or impressive about it.

So if you're interested in transforming your mess, start by listing all the reasons why you dislike having a cluttered desk. Think through the downsides it creates for your own work, and include the way it probably looks to orderly colleagues and bosses.

Then allocate a good chunk of time and start on a big clear-up operation. File or throw away every single sheet of paper – don't leave anything on your desk. If you find that you have a pile of "deal with this today" things, create a suspension file called "To Deal With Today" and file the lot. (And, of course, deal with it later today!) You will probably have to create other files as well – the goal, which is not complicated, is to find a rational home for every piece of paper. If you have to expand your filing system to accomplish this, create a map of the system to remind you of what goes where. When the job's complete, dust and polish your desk, put flowers or a family photograph on it and revel in the clarity and space.

Your goal now is to keep your desk clutter-free. This is easier said than done. It's so simple to fall back into old habits, particularly when you are under pressure. You have to be firm and rigorous with yourself – remember, habits are what you do a lot, and the aim is to replace the old habit of being messy with the new habit of being orderly. Maintenance has one unbreakable law: *don't put it down – put it away or throw it away*. If you keep to this golden rule you'll come to wonder how you ever managed before. I should know – I am the ex-Queen of Clutter.

I'M DROWNING IN EMAILS

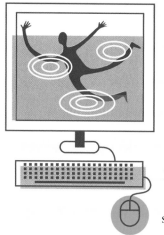
We all know that emails are a marvellously quick and efficient way of sending information, but for some people, they are the bane of their working lives. It's amusing that, in some companies, the volume of emails received is compared almost like a measure of virility, the subtext being "Look how important I am, all these people need to contact me."

However, if your sheer number of emails seems overwhelming, you must take action. If you simply don't reply, the other person is forced to make assumptions why. They're likely to wonder whether it's because you didn't like what you read, or you didn't reply on purpose or you're downright incompetent. This opens the way for misunderstanding.

So you have two main options. One is to allot time to dealing with emails. The phrase "I'll just check my emails," makes it sound like a quick process. But it's not. The only thing that's quick about emails is the speed with which they can be sent. So schedule a realistic amount of time for the task. To avoid "email constipation", it's essential to deal *properly* with each email. This means that you either file it electronically, or print it out and file it, or deal with it and delete it. Regularly delete the emails you've dealt with – it takes only moments. Aim to clear your in-box every day.

The other option is to instigate change. Email is a limited mode of communication. It's one-way, and it's a sterile format. Consider the fact that in face-to-face meetings, eighty per cent of communication is non-verbal. In your team's range of communication tools – meetings, 'phone calls, video-conferences, voice-mail – email is the most low-grade. It's great for transmitting simple facts and data, but it should *not* be used for criticism, brainstorming, firing people or anything where human interaction is necessary.

Few companies have an agreed protocol on the use of email. If yours does not, consider inventing one that can be adopted, if not by the whole company, by your team or department. Before embarking on this, check informally how your colleagues feel; if they, too, are struggling with their emails, you may find a surprising degree of interest.

An agreed protocol on the use of email might include, for example: never sending an email when you can easily walk to discuss a matter with the person or when calling them would be more effective; sending an email only if you want the person to take action (and copying in only those who need to know); finding other ways of communicating – for example, setting up a project intranet for shared information, including an electronic whiteboard and a bulletin board; and, finally, holding frequent meetings to update information and exchange requests in person, rather than electronically.

Everyone needs to agree to comply with the protocol, especially for the first month while new habits are being established. As information about all aspects of the project becomes more easily available, the quality of communication in the team or department should improve, and you will be partially released from the tyranny of your own email inbox.

I'M SURROUNDED BY INEFFECTIVE PEOPLE

Working with ineffective people is absolutely maddening. Ineffectiveness can be a result of inexperience; indecisiveness; weakness; laziness; absenteeism; being in the wrong job – or perhaps the problem lies in the relationship with you.

As a manager you hold some responsibility for understanding why a person working for you is ineffective. You need to work out how they can develop, what support they need, and monitor their development. The other part of the responsibility is held by them.

Always assume that improvement is possible and aim to do a great job of bringing on someone's performance until they become a valued colleague. You need to be thorough in your approach – keep a record of training and meetings in case ultimately you have no option but to dismiss them.

First you need to talk together – in private and without rushing. Don't wait for a performance review to do this – do it when you observe a pattern of ineffectiveness emerging. Tell the person how, in your perception, their performance is falling short. Reassure them that you're committed to providing support to help them improve. Now listen to their side of the story. Don't interrupt; look on this as information-gathering, and try to pinpoint the underlying problem. If the problem seems to lie within your relationship, listen for clues as to why it's going wrong.

If they're simply inexperienced, training or mentoring could help. If they can't make decisions or they're unassertive, they will need your longer-term support (the advice on pp.92–3 and pp.94–7 respectively might help). If they appear lazy, or they're often absent, try to find out why. When you have identified the problem together, agree a way forward. Explain to the person exactly what you require in terms of improved performance and tell them how you will monitor their progress. The other person should keep a record of their achievements too, and you should meet regularly to discuss your findings. Arrange for appropriate help – this might be training or mentoring. Sustain this help until they're developing well. If things are very bad, you must make it clear that unless there is improvement, you will have to dismiss them. Avoid acrimony. Manage your own feelings well; be sympathetic, but firm and clear.

It needn't always be a member of your team that's ineffective. If it is your boss who is ineffective, you will probably feel angry and frustrated and you are probably taking on their job as well as your own. Where you can, delegate upward – give back to your boss work that he or she should be doing (or, ideally, don't accept their workload in the first place). Explain firmly and calmly that you don't have time in your schedule to handle it. Don't badmouth them behind their back. Use your performance review as an opportunity to let your boss know how you would prefer to be managed. If things are really bad, talk to your human resources manager and ask their advice on how the situation can be improved. Again, don't badmouth – talk only about how the problem is affecting *your* productivity.

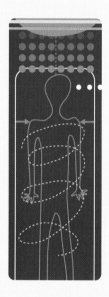

THIS COMPANY DRIVES ME MAD

If something about your company is driving you to distraction, you have three possible courses of action: you could leave (always the last resort); or, you could "quit and stay" – that is, opt to stay on, but simply put no heart in to the job (this is negative and soul-destroying). Or you could try to change the situation (the positive, creative solution).

So, before you start sprucing up your resumé, try to pinpoint exactly what it is that drives you mad. Is it the way the company is structured? Some companies seem to have too many layers of personnel, which can make it hard for individual employees to see clearly how the company operates. In turn, this leads to feelings of detachment and isolation. In large companies, the people who circulate decisions, instructions or objectives can seem out of touch with the actual problems or objectives of most employees and this can cause confusion, resentment and unease.

Has your company grown from small beginnings? Often, during that growth no-one has paused to re-assess the corporate structure, leaving some departments superfluous and others conspicuous by their absence. For example, there might be no Human Resources department because contracts, salaries and expenses are handled by Accounts; whereas hiring and firing, training and complaints procedures come under the auspices of individual department heads (many of whom tend to have little time and no formal training to handle personnel issues). Do you feel that you have no formal structure for confidential complaints? And perhaps no opportunity to discuss your training, performance or salary?

Once you've established where the problem lies, it's time to start putting things right using your skills of assertion, persuasion and compromise. Try drawing a diagram of the people with whom you have contact, and the lines of communication between you all, formal and informal. Highlight your own zone of influence. Let's say that the thing that drives you most mad is that a decision-maker, who needs to make regular assessments about your team's work, is rarely available. Next time you are able to talk to them, explain the problem and ask for a scheduled weekly meeting; or ask if, in their absence, someone else can be given the authority to take decisions. Within your own zone of influence, there is nothing to stop you revamping systems and creating your own relationships and working structures – in fact, once others see how efficiently your department works, the impetus for change and improvement is likely to be catching.

If the company structure makes you feel isolated, unappreciated or detached, find out if anyone would be interested in creating a staff newsletter. Start building a community within your workplace – organize team nights out, or simply lunches. If the problem lies outside your zone of influence, don't dwell on your frustration. Instead, voice your concerns to the person who *can* make a difference. Tell them about the problems and then offer them some possible solutions. Research your solutions thoroughly – especially if they involve financial commitment. If you can, offer to take on some of the responsibility for change yourself and in this way make your own contribution to making things better.

I'M BEING HARASSED

Harassment is any form of unwanted and unwelcome behaviour – ranging from offensive remarks to physical violence – that makes a person feel offended or humiliated. It's judged to be harassment if any reasonable person would have the same response to the behaviour. If the unwanted behaviour is linked to your gender or sexual orientation, it's sexual harassment. If it is linked to your colour, or racial or ethnic background, it's racial harassment.

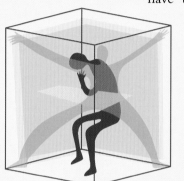

Sexual harassment comes in two forms: "*Quid pro quo*" harassment, which makes conditions of employment (hiring, promotion or retention) dependent on the victim providing sexual favours – for example "Sleep with me or you're fired." The other form, which applies also to racial harassment, is "hostile working environment" – when the perpetrator's words or behaviour are sufficiently offensive to alter the conditions of the victim's employment and create an extremely unpleasant working environment.

Harassment, whether sexual or racial, is not usually a one-off event. "I wake up in the morning", said a young female manager, who was being sexually harassed, "and for a second or two I'm relaxed. But once I remember what awaits me at work, epinephrine (adrenaline) floods my body and I feel too queasy to eat breakfast." She felt angry at the perpetrator, and also at herself for being afraid to confront him.

Over time, harassment can wear down your immune system, leaving you prone to disease. You may also fall into reactive depression. This is not mental illness; it's classed as "psychiatrically injured".

The financial cost of harassment in the workplace is high. Abuse results in accidents and mistakes, increased sick leave, lost productivity, high staff turnover and high recruitment costs. Human resources experts peg the cost of replacing an employee at two to three times the individual's salary.

Companies have a duty to provide a harassment-free working environment. Your employer should have a sexual harassment policy, which includes a system of help and advice, as well as disciplinary and legal remedies.

The moment you realize you're being harassed, begin keeping a detailed record of the harassment, and avoid one-to-one meetings with the perpetrator. The next step is to take firm action, to warn the perpetrator that his or her behaviour is unacceptable. *Don't* meet with them on your own, as you lay yourself open to further abuse. Either deliver the message verbally in the presence of a trusted person, or better still, put it in writing, with a copy to the bully's boss. If the bully *is* your boss, copy the letter to the Chief Executive Officer and the Human Resources department (in fact, make sure your Human Resources department are kept fully informed whoever is harassing you). Be unequivocal about the nature of the harassment, and stress how unwelcome it is. Be brave – most people who are being harassed think that they won't be believed. Remember, your health, dignity and well-being are under threat. Keep in the front of your mind the fact that harassment is not only wretched and offensive – it's illegal.

MY JOB IS UNDER THREAT

There's no doubt that the days of jobs for life are long gone. Unfortunately, in the fast-moving workplace of today, job security can never be taken absolutely for granted. So what can you do if you believe your job may be under threat? First, don't panic! It's important to manage the situation as

positively as possible. Don't take office gossip seriously or rely on the grapevine – you may be worrying about nothing. Depressing discussions based on half-truths get everyone down. Try to find out the facts by asking your boss or line manager for as full a picture as possible.

Worrying about losing your job is very undermining. If you are supporting a family, your worry can translate into real fear, and maybe anger too, particularly if the situation seems unfair. If you feel that you are starting to suffer anxiety or depression, don't try to deal with it alone. Speaking to the right people and making an action plan will help you take charge of the situation. As well as talking to your boss, discuss the situation with your partner, spouse or friends; consulting your financial adviser might be wise, too.

Is it specifically you or your role that's threatened? If it's you, there should be performance assessments available for discussion: do you agree with them? Do you understand any criticisms? Find out exactly why things have got to this stage, and what's needed to move you onto firmer ground. Similarly, if your role or your whole department is under threat, is there anything you can do in terms of retraining or changing role, that will improve your position? Could you be transferred to a different department?

Now get planning. The reality is that in the end it may be necessary to change jobs. Remember that moving jobs is a big life change, and like it or not, you will be thrown into the Change Journey (see pp.46–7). Being well-prepared will reduce the anxiety in the journey.

This is the time to create an impeccable resumé. A resumé is not just a list of your jobs so far, but an important sales tool, so take your time and put effort into it. If necessary seek professional help, as did the young female graduate who had held several unconnected short-term posts with no obvious career path. She was struggling to write a resumé that would get her an interview for the job she wanted, so she sought help from a resumé writer who showed her how to create a truthful and impressive picture of her capabilities. Remember, companies employ new people because they need someone to fulfil a specific role – your resumé should show how *you* fit the bill perfectly.

Also, research the marketplace. Find out about other companies in your field, so that you know the bigger picture. Is there any training that would enhance your saleability? Is this the time to move in a new direction? Networking can lead to opportunities – so ask around. Above all, try to be positive and upbeat. It's vital to take active charge of your well-being at this time, so that you are energized and ready to move forward when your golden opportunity arises.

LEADERSHIP CAN BE LONELY

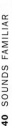
Being a leader of others means, by its very nature, that you must be prepared to stand alone, to bear the burden of heavy responsibility, and to lead others through both good times and bad. As one experienced leader put it, "I'm responsible for so much: my people's jobs, their salaries, their promotions, their families — ultimately, their well-being depends on my judgment."

One of the hardest times for a leader is when you have to keep your own counsel and make a difficult decision. It may be a decision that is received with dismay and resentment, but you are not at liberty to give your staff the complete picture. As a successful leader in his early fifties remarked: "When I want to lean back for support, I can't necessarily expect to find anyone behind me." This is a lonely position in which to find yourself.

There will be times when, as a leader, you have to struggle with uncertainty; times when the most difficult but potentially creative option is to wait and allow yourself to be "lost" for a while, without panicking (see p.44). This is potentially stressful for anyone, but particularly so when the careers and livelihoods of others hang on your decisions.

All the tough aspects of being a leader tend to make us physically tense. It's therefore essential for your well-being and the success of your leadership that you develop expert self-awareness of your thinking habits (see pp.40–43), and of your moment-to-moment bodily tension (see pp.30–33). This will ensure that you are fully present in difficult situations, while simultaneously keeping a grasp of the bigger picture.

Successful leaders must also establish sustaining support structures. If you have the backing of a clear, rigorous decision-making process, this will be hugely supportive of your own thinking. It will underpin the painful or complex decisions, and allow you to check the validity of decisions that have to be made during times of uncertainty. It's helpful, too, in hard times, to remember that no matter how important you are, you still play only a small part in a much larger whole.

Another immensely helpful source of support is to find yourself mentors to whom you can turn in times of need. A trusted mentor can create a replenishing personal forum where you test and develop your thinking. One American company leader told me that he and other leaders, from unrelated companies, formed themselves into a long-standing group whose function was to support one another. This has lasted years, and has proved hugely valuable.

Monitoring your life balance is also vital (see pp.72–5). If you allow yourself to live for work, your perspective is narrowed and your judgment can become subtly limited. Furthermore, your physical health will be more easily undermined. On the other hand, a personal life full of deep and rich experiences can be drawn upon to help sustain the success of your leadership and protect your well-being. Creating *and practising* daily strategies for stress release really is non-optional (and creates a wonderful example for your staff).

chapter 5

QUICK-FIX SOLUTIONS

Any working day contains ups and downs, which can make us feel a whole range of emotions from excitement and satisfaction to boredom and frustration. During difficult days, the tension in our bodies keeps mounting, making us uptight and exhausted. This is why it is a good idea to have a few quick-fix solutions at your fingertips, so that you can continuously release physical tension and keep yourself relaxed, calm and productive.

This chapter provides you with a first-aid kit of just such solutions. Practise these techniques at home with the book beside you, repeating them as many times as it takes you to be able to perform them easily from memory. Then, begin to incorporate them into your work life.

Once these solutions become an integral part of your work routine, you'll find that even after a bad day, instead of going home feeling exhausted and tense you'll feel surprisingly calm and relaxed. This is a huge bonus. You'll no longer take work (trapped in your body) home with you, and you'll have energy left to enjoy your leisure time.

BE YOUR OWN MENTOR

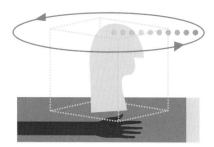

Wouldn't it be handy if in times of stress you had a mentor who would appear magically, and help you see things with clarity and wisdom? Unfortunately few of us have the luxury of such a guiding light, but there is no reason why we can't try to be our own mentor.

One of the first things a mentor would suggest is that you care for yourself properly. So, when faced with a stressful situation your first reaction should be to breathe deeply, as this provides instant first-aid. Then, rationalize the situation. If, for example, you are finding a colleague difficult, remind yourself that even if it doesn't feel like it, you are both working in the best interests of the company. When there is friction, it is sometimes because individual agendas differ – for example, one person is trying to please the client, while another is trying to cut running costs.

Next, examine the true motive behind your own behaviour. For example, you may have rationalized that it's imperative to meet a certain deadline – that's why you're pushing yourself and your team so ruthlessly. But actually the underlying (and real) driver is that if you don't meet this deadline, you will feel a failure – and failure is not an option. By stepping back and analyzing the situation in much the same way as a mentor would, you can often see the bigger picture. However things unfold, tell yourself that you are a person trying his or her best and be compassionate to yourself – and others.

GO FOR A SHORT STROLL

During a pressurized day, it's easy for tension to gather in your body almost imperceptibly. Your shoulders, neck and jaw tighten and your breathing becomes shallow. Consequently your energy levels drop and your thinking loses flexibility and creativity.

The moment you realize that this is happening (see pp.30–33), go for a short stroll alone. If possible, go out in the fresh air for a few moments; if not, it's still helpful just to walk yourself down the corridor. As you stroll, deepen your breathing, and with each outbreath, mindfully drop your shoulders and soften your jaw.

Now focus your attention inward. Notice your feelings, without becoming caught up in them; whether things seem too hectic or too static, remind yourself that everything evolves and changes.

TAKE A SLOW, DEEP BREATH

Have you ever noticed what happens to your breathing when you're angry, upset or frustrated? You most probably take light, shallow breaths. This is all part of the way in which we suppress feelings in difficult situations (for example, in an abrasive meeting, when we're having to contain exasperation). Another time we're likely to breathe minimally is when we've been focusing on a computer screen for a while.

In such situations you can release tension, refresh and relax yourself in moments, by taking a slow, deep breath. Begin by breathing out. Then, sitting straight, breathe in slowly and mindfully: imagine that you're blowing up a balloon in your belly. When you can breathe in no more, release the whole breath by breathing out all your stale tension and fatigue. Practise deep breathing often – it's an instant energizer.

RELEASE NECK TENSION

Have you ever noticed someone in a meeting do one of those sudden, very fast head rotations? Don't do it! I'm going to show you a better way to release tension from your neck, which doesn't risk injury.

This exercise takes a couple of minutes. First, establish a rhythm of slow, deep breathing. Try to visualize that every out-breath is releasing tension from your neck and keep this image in your mind throughout the exercise.

Next, focus your attention on your body. Allow your head to drop forward very slowly. Let the weight of your head gently stretch the back of your neck – you should feel the pull down between your shoulder blades. Slowly come up; then, without forcing anything, gently drop your head toward your left shoulder. Feel the stretch, but don't push it – let the weight of your head lengthen that muscle all on its own. Bring your head back to the centre and then, taking your time, gently drop your head toward the right shoulder. Returning your head to the centre once more, allow your head to drop right back this time. After a few moments in this position, allow your jaw to slacken (if your neck's been tense, the odds are that your jaw has been tight, too).

Finally, raise your head again so that it's back in a central position. You should now feel poised and relaxed. Keep your jaw slack and finish off the exercise with a long, deep breath.

SLIDE YOUR SHOULDERS

Take a moment to assess how you are sitting, right now as you read this book. Focus on the upper body. Are your shoulders up around your ears? We all seem to gather tension across the tops of our shoulders (as well as in the neck, the jaws, the eye sockets and the scalp – it's no wonder that the manufacturers of headache pills never go out of business!). This powerful little exercise will help you to loosen your shoulder muscles. It takes about a minute to do it properly – any less and you're rushing it.

Start by checking exactly how tight your shoulders are feeling. Take a deep breath down into your belly, then release it slowly. Now, lift your shoulders right up to your ears, and hold them there. Notice it's harder to breathe well in this position. Next, very slowly, begin to lower your shoulders, making tiny movements. The slower you do this, the more effective it is. Take a full minute to lower them, and allow your breathing to open up as your shoulders creep down.

If you have done the exercise correctly you should find that your shoulders come down to roughly where you're expecting them to stop – and then they carry on dropping, until they feel as if they are halfway down to your waist! When your shoulders finally do come to rest, take a moment to appreciate the satisfying physical sensation of release, and conclude the exercise with a long, deep, calming breath.

STRETCH YOUR BACK

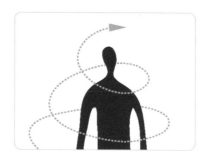

This exercise, which helps to maintain a flexible, pain-free spine, was taught to me by a chiropractor. It takes less than five minutes to do, so try to perform it twice a day if you can.

Begin by sitting on the edge of a chair. Take a deep breath, exhale, and focus all your attention on your body. Raising your left knee, clasp your hands around it, and without forcing the movement, lift up your knee to meet your forehead. Then, lower your knee again. Now repeat the same movement with your right knee.

Repeat this sequence ten times on each side, making sure you stretch your spine but without forcing the movements. You should find that your knees get closer to your forehead with practice.

Now stand up. Put your right hand on your right hip, then lean slowly over to your right. Allow your head to drop to the right as well, so that your whole spine makes a gentle sideways curve. Return to an upright position again and, putting your left hand on your left hip, repeat the whole movement to your left. Do ten repetitions on each side.

Finish the exercise by interlacing your hands and raising them above your head, palms facing the ceiling. Reach upward, feeling your ribs lift and breathing in as you stretch. Try to stretch just a little further, and then gently release your muscles as you exhale.

RELAX YOUR SHOULDERS

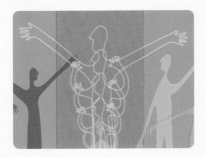

Sometimes it's not until the end of a long, tense day that we realize that our shoulders have become rigid with tension – they feel set in concrete. If you know this happens to you, try these gentle but effective stretches every day. Think of them as a three-minute investment in your well-being.

Stand up straight, your feet hip-distance apart. Take a deep breath, exhale, and focus your attention on your right shoulder. Now, imagine there's a piece of chalk attached to the outside of that shoulder. Breathing deeply and rhythmically, slowly draw five circles in a clockwise direction with the chalk. Start off small and make each circle bigger than the one before it. Then draw five more ever-increasing circles in a counter-clockwise direction. Don't rush. Feel the muscles and ligaments of your shoulder stretch and loosen. Then, repeat the same sequence of movements with your left shoulder.

Now, keeping your arms straight, interlace your fingers behind your back, your palms facing upward. Push your chest forward and pull your shoulders back – feel your chest expand and open.

Conclude the exercise by stretching out the backs of your shoulders. Interlace your hands again and stretch them out in front of you at shoulder height, palms facing away from you. Allow your head to drop forward a little. Now, really push forward into that stretch, and feel how it releases the tightness right across the top of your back.

REGAIN YOUR POISE

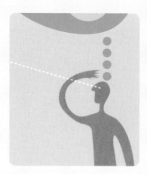

At this moment, without changing a thing and without rushing, check the following three things:

• What is your posture like? Notice where your shoulders are; the curve of your spine; whether or not your feet are planted firmly on the floor.

• How does your current posture affect your breathing? Does it impede you taking a full breath in any way?

• If someone took a picture of you at this moment, what would you be projecting? Energy, poise and calm? Or tension and tiredness?

If any of your answers tended toward the negative side, don't worry. Poor posture is only a habit, and you can change it. Here is an instant solution. Imagine there's a golden thread magically attached to the centre of the top of your head. It leads up into the heavens.

Now allow this golden thread to pull you up as if you were a puppet on a string, so that your whole body feels taller and more poised. Your spine is upright, dignified but relaxed, and your ribcage can expand freely; your shoulders drop into a position of ease, and your head is aligned naturally. Your feet are on the floor, and your arms and hands relaxed.

Now get used to how this new posture feels. Use the golden thread image as often as you like: you will be able to breathe more fully, which will energize you, and you will exude poise, authority, energy and relaxation.

CHECK IN WITH YOUR HEART

Stress inevitably leads to short tempers and frustration, which can damage working relationships. If you find yourself locked in a fruitless argument, or angry or frustrated with a colleague, it's time to check in with your heart.

When we feel negatively toward someone, our body contracts with tension and we speak from our most limited selves. Our vocal chords become tight, strangling our voice, and we don't breathe properly. Our manner may become abrupt or rude.

Your colleagues are the people who can help to relieve your pressure — nourish your relationships with them. When you feel yourself becoming bad-tempered it is worth checking out of the situation for a moment. Take a deep breath and excuse yourself. Notice your negative feelings and then mentally step back from them. Walk around for a minute to regain composure and remind yourself that every human being deserves to be treated with respect.

When you resume your discussion, look directly at the other person, observing them as objectively as possible. Take another deep breath and summon your ethical self and your heart. Apologize for breaking off, and let them have their say. Keep breathing deeply, soften your facial muscles and maintain eye contact. Read their body language — how do you think they are feeling? As you respond kindly, they should visibly relax, which will mean that both of you are in the right frame of mind to resolve the deadlock.

CONCLUSION

For all of us who live pressurized lives, where stress can so easily become a problem, understanding the body-mind connection is a gift beyond price. When you've absorbed what this book offers, you can literally transform your life – and I'm not using the word "transform" lightly. You can develop superb self-awareness, release stress before it settles into debilitating tension, build exceptional energy and well-being – you can open the way to allow your own potential for success to blossom.

This is simple, but not easy: it takes determination. Once you understand why it takes determination, you're much less likely to allow your transformation to be sabotaged.

One of the important themes in this book is that habits consist of behaviour we repeat often and automatically. So to create a new positive habit, you need to practise the new behaviour consciously, many times, until it becomes habitual. The ways you think and act are ingrained after years of having repeated the same things. When you come across an exciting new activity that interests you – for example, a new exercise class or learning meditation – you will probably stick with it at first while your enthusiasm is fresh. But then if you experience a hard, stressful week or two, you might feel distracted, demotivated, or just too plain exhausted to remain keen, and before you know it you slip straight back into old habits.

If you recognize this pattern, now is the time for a life challenge. Ask yourself: "How happy am I with my current way of life? Can I imagine living in a much more relaxed, self-aware, energized way?" If the answers are yes, you need to realize that the power to change your life lies with you – and no-one else. When you're ready, promise yourself: "For the next six weeks (long enough to establish new habits and let go of old ones), I am consciously choosing to put my well-being top of my agenda – come what may."

Then I want to encourage you to put your focus and drive into whichever of the techniques in this book interest you. You may find it helpful to keep a journal to monitor your progress. Begin by writing on one page the way things are at present – the way stress impacts on you, how you feel, your level of fatigue and so on. On a different page, describe the way you want to see yourself in the future, when you are effortlessly practising the techniques in this book – how you will look and feel, your relaxed body and high energy levels, and how this will change your life. These two pages will be your starting point and your realistic, inspirational goal. If, occasionally, you go briefly into default mode and find yourself lapsing back into bad old habits, don't give up – try to work out why you lost direction, so that you can keep yourself more on track in future.

I truly wish you well with your journey. You have the potential to transform yourself. You *can* do it.

Clare Harris

The following titles provide helpful further reading on important themes in this book:

Fontana, D. *Learn to Meditate*, Duncan Baird Publishers (London), 1998 and Chronicle Books (San Francisco), 1999

George, M. *Learn to Relax*, Duncan Baird Publishers (London) and Chronicle Books (San Francisco), 1998

Harrison, E. *Teach Yourself to Meditate*, Judy Piatkus (London), 1994 and Ulysses Press (Berkeley, CA) 2001

Kabat-Zinn, J. *Mindfulness Meditation for Everyday Life*, Judy Piatkus (London), 1994

Pert, C. B. *Molecules of Emotion – Why You Feel the Way You Feel*, Pocket Books, imprint of Simon & Schuster (London and New York), 1999

Roberts, M. *Fitness for Life Manual*, Dorling Kindersley (London and New York), 2002

Roberts, M. *90-Day Fitness Plan*, Dorling Kindersley (London and New York), 2001

van Straten, M., and Griggs, B. *Super Foods*, Dorling Kindersley (London), 1990 and Lothian Publishing Co. (Long Island City, NY and Melbourne, Australia), 2000

Weil, Dr A. *Eating Well for Optimum Health – The Essential Guide to Food, Diet and Nutrition*, Warner Books (London), 2001 and Random House (New York), 2000

Weil, Dr A. *Spontaneous Healing – How to Discover and Enhance Your Body's Natural Ability to Maintain and Heal Itself*, Warner Books (London), 1997 and Ballantine Books, imprint of Random House (New York), 2000

INDEX

ACKNOWLEDGMENTS

The author would like to thank: John Faulkner, Visiting Fellow at the Praxis Centre for Developing Personal Effectiveness at Cranfield School of Management, for his kindness in allowing me to use the Faulkner Life Balance Map; all my friends at the Praxis Centre for Developing Personal Effectiveness at Cranfield School of Management, in particular Sandy Cotter for supporting my work on stress; and Dr Digger Harris, for his boundless generosity with discussion and ideas.

CONTACT THE AUTHOR

If you would like to share your experiences of using techniques suggested in this book, or if you require any further information about my work, you can contact me at: clareharris@companyathlete.com.